MORE GRACE
MORE
FAVOR

Shippensburg, PA

RELEASING THE UNTAPPED POWER
OF HUMILITY IN YOUR LIFE

MORE GRACE

MORE

FAVOR

Andrew Wommack

Published by Harrison House Publishers
Shippensburg, PA 17257

ISBN 13 TP: 978-1-6803-1523-3

ISBN 13 eBook: 978-1-6803-1524-0

ISBN 13 HC: 978-1-6803-1526-4

ISBN 13 LP: 978-1-6803-1525-7

For Worldwide Distribution, Printed in the U.S.A.

1 2 3 4 5 6 7 8 / 24 23 22 21 20

CONTENTS

Introduction 7

Chapter 1   A Different System 11

Chapter 2   The Curse of Pride 19

Chapter 3   A Trap Called Self-Centeredness 29

Chapter 4   The Pull of Self-Promotion 39

Chapter 5   The Root of Disobedience 47

Chapter 6   What God Requires 55

Chapter 7   The Response of Humility 63

Chapter 8   The Face of Humility 71

Chapter 9   The Results of Humility 79

Chapter 10   Humility Obeys 87

Chapter 11   God's Kind of Love 95

Chapter 12   Humility Is Dependence 103

Chapter 13   A Faithful Witness 111

Chapter 14 The Key to Promotion. 119

Chapter 15 Jesus—Our Example. 127

Chapter 16 True Success 137

Chapter 17 God's Choice 145

Chapter 18 Humility Gives Thanks. 153

Chapter 19 Humility Glorifies God 161

Chapter 20 Humility Defuses Anger. 169

Chapter 21 Judge Not? 177

Chapter 22 Humility Is Merciful. 187

Chapter 23 A Daily Commitment. 195

Chapter 24 Humility and Faith. 203

Chapter 25 Humility Is Consistent 211

Chapter 26 Grace in Time of Need. 219

       Receive Jesus as Your Savior 227

       Receive the Holy Spirit. 229

       About the Author 231

INTRODUCTION

M any years ago, I prayed, "Lord, what do I have to do to get from where I am to where You want me to be?" As I opened my eyes, I saw my Bible in front of me and heard the Lord say, "Put My Word in your heart; it will do the rest."

Since that day, I have discovered that the Word of God is the single most important component of a fruitful and victorious Christian life. It is how we know God (John 1:1) and how we learn to live in the abundant life Jesus came to provide (John 10:10). The Word is our sure foundation. Unfortunately, most Christians don't let the Bible get in the way of what they believe—and it's destroying them. They're selfish and insecure. Like their unsaved neighbors, they're sick, depressed, and

"I have discovered that the Word of God is the single most important component of a fruitful and victorious Christian life."

defeated. Their lives are a wreck because they don't know God. They don't know His Word.

Whether you realize it or not, God's kingdom operates differently than this world's system. It's governed by different laws and different principles, and it gets different results. When the world cowers in fear and terror, God's kingdom is at rest and peace. When the world reels in financial crisis or stumbles through political upheaval, the kingdom of God is prosperous and secure. Romans says the kingdom of God is *"not meat and drink; but righteousness, and peace, and joy in the Holy Ghost"* (Rom. 14:17). The good news is, every born-again person automatically belongs to this kingdom (Col. 1:13); but believers can live their entire lives without experiencing its benefits if they don't know how God's kingdom operates.

The kingdom of God is a kingdom of grace. We don't deserve to be a part of it. We could never earn its benefits. But because of Jesus, we can receive them by faith (Rom. 5:2). What most Christians misunderstand is that faith is more than just believing. Faith is active (James 2:19–20). It responds to the grace of God with humble obedience—obedience to His Word (John 14:21).

The Word of God reveals the laws of God's kingdom. One of those laws is humility. Now, I know humility is not a popular topic today, but humility is close to God's heart. It's part of His character. Jesus, God manifest in the flesh (John 1:14), called Himself meek and lowly in heart (Matt. 11:29). He was humble. And He was a perfect representation of the Father (Heb.

1:3), which means God is humble. He responds to humility. James 4:6 says, *"But he giveth more grace. Wherefore he saith, God resisteth the proud, but giveth grace unto the humble."*

Humility allows us to receive grace from God. The world doesn't understand this, and to a large degree the church doesn't either. They want to operate in grace and experience the favor, ability, and anointing of God, but they don't understand how God thinks about humility.

I pray that this cannot be said of you after reading this book! In the following pages, I'll share the overwhelming scriptural evidence for humility. It is evidence that has transformed my life. If you'll let it, it will transform yours as well. Be blessed.

Chapter One

A DIFFERENT SYSTEM

The kingdom of God is a kingdom of grace. All that God is and has is offered to us in Christ on an unearned, undeserved basis (Rom. 12:6). Unfortunately, many believers live their entire lives without experiencing the benefits of that grace. They simply are not taught to respond to God's grace in faith.

Most people define grace as unmerited favor, and while that definition is correct, it is not complete. The Bible uses the word *grace* to describe many different things. Paul said his ministry to the Gentiles was a *"dispensation"* (or administration) of grace (Eph. 3:2). Then in Romans, he listed gifts of grace (Rom. 12:6–8). The apostle Peter said that we are to use our gifts as *"stewards of the manifold grace of God"* (1 Pet. 4:10). The word *manifold* means, "having many different forms or elements." So, the word *grace* describes not only God's unmerited favor but also His ability, anointing, and power at work in our lives. In short, grace is anything good that comes from God.

> **" So, the word grace describes not only God's unmerited favor but also His ability, anointing, and power at work in our lives."**

Titus 2:11 says that grace has appeared to all people, but not all people receive it. You have to humble yourself to receive what God has provided. We humble ourselves when we receive salvation through what Jesus did for us and not what we do for Him. James 4:6 says we must continue to humble ourselves to receive *"more grace"* to live as He intends:

> *But he giveth more grace. Wherefore he saith, God resisteth the proud, but giveth grace unto the humble.*

The Amplified Bible, Classic Edition translates James 4:6 like this:

> *But He gives us more and more grace (power of the Holy Spirit, to meet this evil tendency and all others fully). That is why He says, God sets Himself against the proud and haughty, but gives grace [continually] to the lowly (those who are humble enough to receive it).*

Notice that God gives *"more and more grace"* to *"those who are humble enough to receive it."* It takes humility to receive the grace of God. But if we can receive more grace, then it must also be possible to receive less grace. So, while God makes grace available to every person, we choose how much of His grace we experience.

As a believer, you may desire good things in your life. You may be praying for your marriage or your kids. You may have "health and wealth" scriptures posted on your mirror or be repeating what you've heard your pastor say from the pulpit. But if you lack humility, you will limit the grace of God in your life. You won't have any less of His Spirit living in you (Col. 1:9–10), but you'll have less of His Spirit flowing through you. You'll be saved and *stuck*. You must learn to cooperate with the laws of God's kingdom and choose to do things God's way to experience the fullness of His grace.

The kingdom of God operates on a different system than this world. When Jesus saw how invited guests were picking seats of honor at a feast at a Pharisee's house, He advised them to take a place of lesser honor. Because, if someone more important were to attend, their host would not be forced to humiliate them by moving them to a different seat. Instead, the host might offer them a seat of greater honor in front of all the guests. *"For whosoever exalteth himself shall be abased; and he that humbleth himself shall be exalted"* (Luke 14:11). You know, I go to ministers' conferences and see this all the time. People jockey for position to get close to influential ministers, to be recognized, or to get the best seat. But Jesus said to not exalt yourself or expect special treatment and attention in those types of situations.

This is the opposite of how the world thinks. The world says things like, "Look out for number one," "If I don't promote myself, who will," and "Take it—you deserve it." Most of the people gracing our magazine covers or running for public office live this way. They are arrogant, selfish, and rude. They believe life's greatest tribute is to say, "I made it on my own. I did it my way." But the Word of God says this is a great deception.

> *The way of man is not in himself: it is not in man that walketh to direct his steps.*
>
> **Jeremiah 10:23**

> *For all that is in the world, the lust of the flesh, and the lust of the eyes, and the pride of life, is not of the Father, but is of the world.*
>
> **1 John 2:16**

This world's system is separated from God. It's not *"of the Father."* Unfortunately, many Christians still operate in the world's system of pride and independence. As believers, we are no longer of this world; we are new creatures in Christ (2 Cor. 5:17). We should not be living like the world. We shouldn't even think like they do. As new creations, we have new natures—natures that no longer crave sin. *Then why do I still struggle with sin and selfishness?* some ask themselves. They read the Word yet see their own shortcomings and think they must have two natures. One nature loves God and wants to do right, while the other wars against those godly desires. This is simply not true.

As Paul declared in Romans, your old nature—that part of you drawn to sin—died. It was crucified with Christ.

> *Knowing this, that our old man is crucified with him, that the body of sin might be destroyed, that henceforth we should not serve sin. For he that is dead is freed from sin. Now if we be dead with Christ, we believe that we shall also live with him: knowing that Christ being raised from the dead dieth no more; death hath no more dominion over him. For in that he died, he died unto sin once: but in that he liveth, he liveth unto God. Likewise reckon ye also yourselves to be dead indeed unto sin, but alive unto God through Jesus Christ our Lord.*

Romans 6:6–11

Paul said that just like Christ died to sin and was resurrected to glorify God, we too become dead to sin but *"alive unto God"* when we believe. The old nature, our "old man," died. The new nature 2 Corinthians 5:17 talks about now lives to glorify God, just like Jesus did. This doesn't mean Christians are incapable of sinning. It means we don't have to be controlled by sin.

Christ's love controls us. Since we believe that Christ died for all, we also believe that we have all died to our old life.

2 Corinthians 5:14, New Living Translation

We now have a choice: we can allow Christ's love to control us, or we can continue to allow our old habits and opinions to direct our lives. You see, God made the mental, soulish part of us similar to a computer. We can program our minds so that certain actions and attitudes become automatic. Before salvation, we were all programed to put self first. The reason most Christians continue to struggle with sin is that they haven't reprogrammed these attitudes. They haven't renewed their minds.

❬❬ We now have a choice: we can allow Christ's love to control us, or we can continue to allow our old habits and opinions to direct our lives."

The sin nature used to rule our thinking. It taught us to be selfish, to fear and hate. Christ broke the power of that nature, but those old habits still have to be dealt with. Just like a computer continues to act on its programming until that programming is changed, our minds continue to lead us into sin until they are renewed (Rom. 12:2).

This is the point Paul was making in Romans. To experience the life of Christ and glorify God, we must recognize that the old self is dead. And we must take steps to renew our minds to the truth of who we now are, until those old actions and attitudes are "reprogrammed." We must disconnect from this world's influence so we can operate in God's kingdom.

Just like there are physical laws that govern the earth, so there are spiritual laws that govern the kingdom of God. Learning to operate within those laws allows us to experience more of His kingdom. For example, God created gravity for our good. It keeps us from floating off into space and holds our cars safely in their own lanes. But if someone goes against that law and steps off a building or drives off a bridge, the same law God created to bless them can kill them. God doesn't hate them. He's not against them. It's just a law of physics.

The same is true of electricity. Though the laws that govern electricity haven't changed since the Garden of Eden, it has taken us thousands of years to discover how to use electricity properly. It wasn't until fairly recently that we began to understand that electricity doesn't flow through all materials the same. It may be easy for a woodworker, like me, to build a lamp out of wood, but I'll only frustrate myself if I expect that lamp to light my house without first hooking up a copper wire to conduct the electricity. I can't blame God for not giving me light. I haven't cooperated with His laws.

❝ If you feel stuck or like everything in life is falling apart, maybe you aren't cooperating with the laws of God.❞

Humility is a spiritual law that governs God's kingdom. Trying to live outside that law will only set you up for frustration. If you feel stuck or like everything in life is falling apart, maybe you aren't cooperating with the laws of God.

Proverbs 15:33 says, *"The fear of the LORD is the instruction of wisdom; and before honour is humility."* In God's kingdom, grace and honor don't work outside humility. You need to learn what true humility is so you can begin cooperating with it.

Chapter Two

THE CURSE OF PRIDE

Though much of the church world doesn't understand biblical humility, most agree humility is the opposite of pride. God hates pride (Prov. 6:16–19). Proverbs 13:10 says, *"Only by pride cometh contention."* All contention, anger, and strife—and the resulting bitterness—is a direct result of pride (Prov. 17:14).

Proverbs 18:12 says, *"Before destruction the heart of man is haughty, and before honour is humility."* This echoes what Solomon said in Proverbs 16:18: *"Pride goeth before destruction, and an haughty spirit before a fall."* The main reason people struggle in life is pride. It's why they run through marriages and careers, why they struggle financially, and why their health is failing.

That's not to say every problem we face is caused by our pride; our problems can be caused by another person's pride. But most human suffering is self-imposed. It comes as a direct result of refusing to humble ourselves before God and follow His wisdom.

❝But most human suffering is self-imposed. It comes as a direct result of refusing to humble ourselves before God and follow His wisdom.❞

People often come to me for prayer in the area of finances. And inevitably, after spending time with them, I discover that they have plenty of money coming in; they simply overspend. Instead of following the wisdom of the Word and saving for the things they want, they indulge themselves and purchase everything on credit. They end up paying two or three times in interest what an item is worth—and they know better! They know how interest works. They know they shouldn't spend money they don't have. But they want it *now*. So, they override wisdom in the name of instant gratification. That's pride.

You may not realize it, but pride is the original sin. Even before Adam and Eve's sin in the Garden of Eden destroyed the human race, pride got Lucifer kicked out of heaven:

> *How art thou fallen from heaven, O Lucifer, son of the morning! how art thou cut down to the ground, which didst weaken the nations! For thou hast said in thine heart, I will ascend into heaven, I will exalt my throne above the stars of God: I will sit also upon the mount of the congregation, in the*

> *sides of the north: I will ascend above the heights of the clouds; I will be like the most High.*

Isaiah 14:12–14

Lucifer didn't hate God; he envied God. He wanted to *"ascend into heaven."* He wanted to be exalted *"like the most High."* Ezekiel called Lucifer an *"anointed cherub."* He said Lucifer was covered in precious stones with tambourines and pipes built into him (Ezek. 28:13–14). Most scholars believe Satan was created as heaven's worship leader. They say his body literally made music. But Satan was not content to be what God designed him for; he wanted the glory and worship reserved for God. That's pride.

Adam and Eve fell into the same trap. When they ate of the Tree of the Knowledge of Good and Evil, they didn't hate God. They wanted to be like Him. So, they rejected God's wisdom and exalted their own. Most people call this disobedience, but it is, at its core, pride. Eve thought God was keeping something from her. She thought He was denying her some blessing. So, she leaned to her own understanding (Prov. 3:5) to get that blessing her own way. She became independent of God.

All God denied Adam and Eve was the hurt, heartache, death, sickness, and poverty that would come because of sin. Sin would not have happened if Adam and Eve had said, "It's not up to me to pick and choose when to trust God. God is good. God is God, and I am not. This is what He said, so I'm going to obey." In other words, if they had humbled them-selves and exalted God's wisdom above their own wisdom, they wouldn't have sinned.

Adam and Eve had no reason to doubt God. He'd never been anything but good to them. They lived in a perfect world. There was plenty of food. There was no pain, and there were no problems. They literally lived in paradise. There was no reason for them to think God was withholding something. But pride drove them to sin. Pride started all the evil and corruption in this world, and it is still driving us into sin. All sin is rooted in pride.

Society has put a premium on pride, and because the church has not truly understood or taught humility, many believers conform to the world's pattern of pride—or false humility—by default. Scripture tells us to live one way, but we say, "No, I'm going to live like this." We want a godly end, but we do ungodly things. Though the Word says not to be unequally yoked with an unbeliever, thousands violate that principle when choosing a mate (2 Cor. 6:14). Instead of choosing a life partner whose core values and beliefs mimic their own, many people choose a mate based only on outward appearance. Men are attracted to long, wavy hair and a curvy figure, not realizing those curves will fill in after two or three children. Women look for a tall, dark, and handsome man. But when that man experiences Dunlop disease and his belly has done lopped over his belt buckle, they fall out of "love." That's not love. That's lust. And it's prideful.

Proverbs 22:4 declares, *"By humility and the fear of the LORD are riches, and honour, and life."* And while I'm certain every person reading this book desires riches, honor, and life, not many are humbling themselves to receive it. Not many are looking to God's Word for life. The Word says that the person who desires a good, long life must keep their tongue from evil and pursue peace (Ps. 34:12–14). It also says, *"A merry heart doeth good like a medicine"* (Prov. 17:22) and *"Honour thy father and thy mother"* (Ex. 20:12). That means there is a spiritual side to health.

This is just Andyology, but I think diet and exercise are only a small percentage of overall health—maybe twenty or thirty percent. That's not to say we can eat junk food and become couch potatoes. No one will prosper living that way. But working out five hours a day and not touching red meat isn't all there is to

> **❝ They set aside God's wisdom to exalt their own and spend the rest of their lives trying to mitigate the consequences. Most people wouldn't see that as pride, but it is. ❞**

health either. Many people follow "health rules" religiously, but they're bitter and angry, harboring unforgiveness in their hearts. They curse themselves and others, not understanding that *"death and life are in the power of the tongue"* (Prov. 18:21). They set aside God's wisdom to exalt their own and spend the rest of their lives trying to mitigate the consequences. Most people wouldn't see that as pride, but it is. And that pride frustrates the grace of God. Paul said:

If you have died with Christ to the world's way of doing things, why do you let others tell you how to live? It's as though you were still under the world's influence.

**Colossians 2:20,
God's Word**

We shouldn't feel completely at home in this world. We should live as *"strangers and pilgrims on the earth"* (Heb. 11:13), knowing that our real home is in heaven. That doesn't mean we don't experience fulfilled lives. We simply choose to live God's way. The apostle James declared:

Ye adulterers and adulteresses, know ye not that the friendship of the world is enmity with God? whosoever therefore will be a friend of the world is the enemy of God. Do ye think that the scripture saith in vain, The spirit that dwelleth in us lusteth to envy?

James 4:4–5

Those are strong words. But they're New Testament scripture. People often misunderstand this passage. They hear the word *lusteth* and automatically equate it with sin. But *lusteth* as it is used here simply means to have a strong desire. Lust doesn't have to be sinful. A person can lust after a doughnut.

People also incorrectly believe that the subject of verse 5 is the human spirit. In reality, this verse is talking about the Spirit of God. Look at verse 5 again in another translation:

> *Or do you suppose that the Scripture is speaking to no purpose that says, The Spirit Whom He has caused to dwell in us yearns over us and He yearns for the Spirit [to be welcome] with a jealous love?*

James 4:5, AMPC

This scripture isn't talking about our spirits lusting after the world; it's talking about the Spirit of God yearning over us, desiring for us to be completely committed to Him. Exodus 34:14 says that our God is a *"jealous God"* and like a loving husband, God doesn't want to share us with every man on the block. He wants us for Himself. He wants us to love Him and love His values. God doesn't want us to adopt or embrace the values of this world. We become like adulterers and adulteresses when we love all that is in and of this world. When we glorify greed and entertain ourselves with violence and sensuality, and when we celebrate homosexuality and ignore the murder of innocent children, we commit spiritual adultery. That's pride.

Look at James 4 again:

> *But he giveth more grace. Wherefore he saith, God resisteth the proud, but giveth grace unto the*

humble. Submit yourselves therefore to God. Resist
the devil, and he will flee from you.

James 4:6–7

Verse 7 isn't inserted out of context. This passage is still talking about the relationship between humility and pride. It's saying that when we humble ourselves and submit to God, deferring to God and following His leading instead of our own wisdom, we receive the strength—the grace—we need to resist the devil. Rebuking and quoting Scripture is not all there is to resisting the devil. Resisting pride is resisting the devil.

The word *resist* basically means to actively fight against. You cannot be passive about pride. You cannot think, *What's the big deal?* or *Everyone has pride.* You must actively fight against the devil—against pride—by humbling and submitting yourself to God. Pride is the opposite of who God is. Amos 3:3 says, "[How] *can two walk together, except they be agreed?*" When we choose to go our own way and walk in pride, we're walking in opposition to God. God is not personally against us, but He can't walk with us or we'd both be going the wrong way!

❛❛ You must actively fight against the devil—against pride— by humbling and submitting yourself to God."

James 4 goes on to say, "*Draw nigh to God, and he will draw nigh to you*" (James 4:8). How do you "*draw nigh*" to God? You humble yourself (James 4:10). Psalm 138:6 says, "*Though the Lord be high, yet hath he respect unto the lowly: but the proud he knoweth afar off.*" In other words, God stays away from pride. That's part of pride's curse. Prideful people can't have intimacy with God. The second book of Samuel recorded one of David's songs, saying:

> *With the merciful thou wilt shew thyself merciful, and with the upright man thou wilt shew thyself upright. With the pure thou wilt shew thyself pure; and with the froward thou wilt shew thyself unsavoury. And the afflicted people thou wilt save: but thine eyes are upon the haughty, that thou mayest bring them down.*

> **2 Samuel 22:26–28**

If you're frustrated with life, or if you're not seeing your prayers answered or the good things of God manifest, it could be that pride is repelling the grace of God. First Timothy 3 lists the qualifications of an elder. It says that an elder should not be a *"novice, lest being lifted up with pride he fall into the condemnation of the devil"* (1 Tim. 3:6). Many think this scripture means that Satan condemns people when they fall into pride. But this is saying that if we're lifted up in pride, if we go our own way or tie the manifestation of God's power to our own goodness and wisdom, we join in the devil's condemnation. We partake of the same punishment he received when he was cast out of God's presence. Pride has been cursed; it's been condemned. Stop operating in pride and start walking in the same direction as God. God resists the proud. It's not personal. It's a law of the kingdom.

Chapter Three

A TRAP CALLED SELF-CENTEREDNESS

It breaks my heart to see the number of Spirit-filled believers using the Word of God as a magic token to fulfill their selfish desires. They hear that the Gospel says we've been made righteous, and we've been prospered and healed. They hear that we can have peace and joy, that God delights to bless us and give us the desires of our hearts. And while all that is true, those blessings are not why we love and serve God. We love God because He first loved us (1 John 4:19). We serve God because He is God (Ps. 100:3). These believers forget that God has already met our eternal need in Christ and that He promised to meet our physical needs when we seek first His kingdom (Matt. 6:33). They don't understand that blessings come as a byproduct of serving God. They are not the goal.

Self-centeredness lays a trap that way too many people fall into. Society blinds them to the danger by celebrating

❝ But I'm telling you, if you're all wrapped up in yourself, you make a very small package. It's impossible to be truly happy and find fulfilment in life as a selfish, self-centered person.❞

self-centeredness as independence and self-reliance. Humility is reviled. But I'm telling you, if you're all wrapped up in yourself, you make a very small package. It's impossible to be truly happy and find fulfilment in life as a selfish, self-centered person. Selfishness is like a dope addiction. A person focused on satisfying their own needs and desires can never get enough. There is always something more to entice them—a new car, a bigger house, a better job, a younger mate. They spend all their efforts striving for more, but once they get it, the excitement wears off and they need another something to create that emotional high.

Most of us live in an infinitely better house than our parents and grandparents had. We drive nicer cars; we own nicer things. We have so much stuff, but we aren't satisfied. That's because you can never satisfy self. You have to deny it. You have to make humility the goal and learn to live for something bigger than yourself. Jesus said:

> *For whosoever will save his life shall lose it; but whosoever shall lose his life for my sake and the gospel's, the same shall save it.*
>
> **Mark 8:35**

Similarly, Matthew 10:39 records Jesus as saying, *"He that findeth his life shall lose it: and he that loseth his life for my sake shall find it."* Living a life focused on self will ultimately lead to loss. In Daniel 4, King Nebuchadnezzar had a dream. He dreamed of a tree that covered the whole earth. It was strong and beautiful. Its branches reached into heaven, and its fruit fed the entire world. An angel appeared in Nebuchadnezzar's dream and said, "Cut the tree down. Strip its leaves. Scatter its fruit. But put a band of iron around its stump. Let it feel the dew of heaven and live amongst the animals for seven years." The dream disturbed Nebuchadnezzar, and he called his wise men to interpret it.

Daniel, one of the king's wise men, said, "King Nebuchadnezzar, you are that tree. Your kingdom has encompassed the whole earth, but it will be cut down. And you will become like a wild animal for seven years, living amongst the beasts of the field, eating grass like an ox, and feeling the dew of heaven upon your back." Daniel told Nebuchadnezzar that this judgment would last until he learned *"that the most High ruleth in the kingdom of men, and giveth it to whomsoever he will"* (Dan. 4:25). Daniel encouraged the king to humble himself before God; but Nebuchadnezzar didn't listen.

One day as Nebuchadnezzar was out walking on the roof of the royal palace, he said, *"Is not this* [the] *great Babylon, that I have built . . . by the might of my power, and for the honour of my majesty?"* (Dan. 4:30). Scripture says that while the words were still in his mouth, God judged Nebuchadnezzar's pride, and he became like a wild animal. For seven years the king lived outside among the beasts. His hair grew like fur. His nails became like claws, and he ate grass like the oxen. At the end of the seven years, Nebuchadnezzar's mind was restored, and he said:

> *And at the end of the days I Nebuchadnezzar lifted up mine eyes unto heaven, and mine understanding returned unto me, and I blessed the most High, and I praised and honoured him that liveth for ever, whose dominion is an everlasting dominion, and his kingdom is from generation to generation . . . Now I Nebuchadnezzar praise and extol and honour the King of heaven, all whose works are truth, and his ways judgment: and those that walk in pride he is able to abase.*

Daniel 4:34 and 37

What an understatement! Here's a man, arguably the most powerful man on the planet—he's conquered the known world, amassed gold and silver, possibly built the Hanging Gardens of Babylon, and erected a sixty-foot statue of himself—who is summarizing his humiliation by saying, *"Those that walk in pride* [God] *is able to abase."*

Brothers and sisters, God did not create us to live our lives focused on self.

Self-centeredness is the root of all grief. It turns wants into needs and needs into personal crises. It destroys relationships and warps good intentions. And most believers don't know how to deal with it. They try praying about and rebuking self. They try shaming self. They try starving self. But nothing they do gets rid of self.

I used to spend my morning prayer time trying to kill self, but all I ended up doing was resurrecting it. I'd confess my sins or pray for God to use me, not realizing I was wasting all my devotion time focused on self. I had to learn to shift my focus—to make myself a living sacrifice. In Romans 12:1, Paul said:

> *I beseech you therefore, brethren, by the mercies of God, that ye present your bodies a living sacrifice, holy, acceptable unto God, which is your reasonable service.*

Self-sacrifice is every believer's reasonable service. But self-sacrifice is hard. It requires humility. We have to shift our focus off self and remember what Paul wrote in Galatians 2:20:

> *I am crucified with Christ: nevertheless I live; yet not I, but Christ liveth in me: and the life which I now live in the flesh I live by the faith of the Son of God, who loved me, and gave himself for me.*

As believers, we are crucified with Christ. Our lives are not our own. They're not about us. In order to be true representatives of Christ, we have to learn to live *"by the faith of the Son of God."* If God believes we can heal the brokenhearted, forgive our families, and love our enemies, we need to humble ourselves and believe it too.

There was a time, when I first began understanding these things, that I prayed, "God, make me humble." But as I searched Scripture, I realized humility is a voluntary thing. God won't make you humble. You have to humble yourself. He can humiliate you (as He did with Nebuchadnezzar), but you have to humble yourself.

> *Humble yourselves in the sight of the Lord, and he shall lift you up.*
>
> **James 4:10**

Jesus understood humility. When He asked His disciples "Who do people say I am?" Peter responded, *"Thou art the Christ, the Son of the living God"* (Matt. 16:16). Jesus blessed him, but when Peter opened his mouth again, Jesus had to rebuke his pride. While Jesus was preparing His disciples for the next phase of His ministry, He began telling them how He would be rejected and mistreated by the elders. He told them that He would die but then rise again. Peter didn't like what Jesus had to say: *"Be it far from thee, Lord: this shall not be unto thee"* (Matt. 16:22). Peter said, "No, Lord; this won't happen.

You'll not be rejected and killed. We won't let it happen. We'll defend you."

Most people think Peter's words were those of a true friend. But Jesus rebuked him, saying, *"Get thee behind me, Satan: thou art an offence unto me: for thou savourest not the things that be of God, but those that be of men"* (Matt. 16:23). In other words, Peter was ignorant of God's will. He was selfishly exalting his own desire over God's plan. Peter didn't understand that Jesus had to die. He didn't understand God's will for Jesus to suffer to keep us from suffering. Jesus bore our judgment and separation to bring us to the Father.

I'm sure it hurt Peter's feelings when Jesus called him Satan, but Jesus had to deal with that pride quickly before it could become a root in His own heart. You may think I'm being sacrilegious when

> **❝Peter was ignorant of God's will. He was selfishly exalting his own desire over God's plan.❞**

I say Jesus had to deny self, but Hebrews says He was tempted in all things as we are, yet without sin (Heb. 4:15). Jesus didn't want to be rejected. He didn't want to suffer pain (Matt. 26:39). But He knew that He had come to die (Rev. 13:8). Jesus couldn't allow His mind to dwell on any other path than the one His Father had set before Him. That would have been pride. Jesus had to humble Himself and rebuke His natural tendency of self-preservation so He could fulfill God's plan for His life (Phil. 2:8).

If we want to fulfill the plans and purposes of God in our own lives, we have to choose to humble ourselves too. Self-centeredness is a trap. Proverbs 29:23 says, *"A man's pride shall bring him low: but honour shall uphold the humble in spirit."* Walking in pride—living life focused on self—will bring us low and hinder what God can do in and through our lives.

Many years ago, Jamie and I traveled to Ohio to minister. It was my second trip to this church, and I was looking forward to another meeting with them. But when the pastor picked us up in an expensive rental car, I could tell something was wrong. It felt strange; the pastor was distant. He took us to a suite of rooms at a different hotel than I'd stayed in the last time I visited. He bought gifts for our boys (who were young and traveling with us) and had stocked the hotel room with an ice chest full of sodas and water bottles. He took us to expensive restaurants and waited on us hand and foot. It was way over the top! At one point he asked where we'd like to eat, and my boys shouted, "McDonald's!" He said, "Oh, no. I could never take you there." It was so strange, so different from the last time we'd been together.

Toward the end of the week, this pastor finally came clean. "I'm sorry for the way I've been treating you," he said. "We had another minister in not long ago who criticized me over the way I treated him. He was upset that I picked him up in my family car instead of renting a limo. He checked out of the hotel I put him in and got a suite of rooms at another hotel. He demanded I provide him with fruit and drinks each day, and he refused to eat anywhere that cost less than twenty-five dollars per plate. Having him was so burdensome, I decided not to invite any more guest speakers to our church, but you were already on the calendar."

He continued apologizing to me about going overboard until I interrupted, "Look, I appreciate what you do to make my visits enjoyable, but I don't mind riding in your car or eating at McDonald's. I don't mind staying in a regular hotel room. I don't want to be a burden to you. I came here to bless you."

Sadly, many ministers project a wrong image of Jesus to the world. It is true that the laborer is worthy of his hire (Luke 10:7) but we should represent the Father the way Jesus did. He was meek and lowly of heart (Matt. 11:29). He didn't come to serve Himself but to serve us (John 13:13-17). We need to humble ourselves and receive the blessings the Lord sends our way, but we need to be humble enough not to promote ourselves (James 4:10; 1 Pet. 5:6).

Brothers and sisters, life is not all about us. We are blessed to be a blessing (Deut. 8:18). We're not to live selfishly and heap all the benefits of grace upon ourselves until they stink of abuse. We must humble ourselves and shift our focus to others. Only then will we find true life.

Chapter Four

THE PULL OF SELF-PROMOTION

Most people won't humble themselves and trust God to exalt them in His timing (1 Pet. 5:6). In their hearts, they know life is more than corporate success and a larger paycheck, but they sacrifice their families, their health, and their consciences to ensure their own promotion. They don't put God first. They worship the almighty dollar. Colossians calls that idolatry (Col. 3:5).

The former CEO of our ministry, Paul Milligan, used to work in product development for a large corporation. Unfortunately, one of his supervisors began stealing Paul's ideas and presenting them to management as his own. Paul's ideas caused the company to prosper, but he never got credit for them. Instead of allowing that injustice to change his attitude, Paul continued to work as to the Lord, trusting that God would reward him. Nearly a year later, Paul was promoted after his supervisor's actions were discovered and his humility during that period was cited as one of the reasons he received the promotion. Paul resisted the pull of self-promotion, and God exalted his humility.

You don't have to stab someone in the back to be promoted. You don't have to manipulate the truth to ensure others see you in the most favorable light. Exodus 20:16 says, *"Thou shalt not bear false witness against thy neighbor."* Bearing false witness is different from lying. People who bear false witness present information in a way that skews its meaning to match their personal agenda. Politicians and salespeople do it all the time. If a salesperson compares their top-of-the-line model to a competitor's base model, they may convince you to pay more for a product that isn't much different than others on the market. Nothing that the salesperson said was technically a lie, but they bore false witness.

Self-promotion is a quick ticket to humiliation. Proverbs says when we promote self and are full of pride, we will be brought low (Prov. 16:18).

Years ago I remember watching a young professional athlete's career being highlighted on the national stage. He'd won a title and signed several endorsement deals. He even had a dance named after him. But this young man had become very prideful. Days before the biggest game of his career, he was promoting himself and slandering his competition on every major network in the country. (Brothers and sisters, when you see that kind of arrogance and self-promotion, I guarantee it's a prelude to disaster.) Everyone thought this athlete would win, but his team was beaten so badly, all he could do during the postgame news conference was pout. He refused to look at anyone and finally walked out. He was completely humiliated.

> *Pride goeth before destruction, and an haughty spirit before a fall. Better it is to be of an humble spirit with the lowly, than to divide the spoil with the proud.*

Proverbs 16:18–19

During the first century, the apostle Paul installed Timothy as head of the church at Ephesus (1 Tim. 1:3). Some scholars believe the church at Ephesus was one of the largest churches of that time. Some estimate it had as many as 100,000 people. After appointing Timothy to pastor all those people, Paul told him not to let anyone despise him because of his youth. *"Be an example to the believers in word, in conduct, in love, in spirit, in faith, in purity"* (1 Tim. 4:12, New King James Version). In other words, he instructed Timothy to earn their respect. You can't force people to respect you or treat you a certain way. Respect is earned.

I find it interesting that Paul didn't tell the people of Ephesus to respect Timothy. Paul founded that church. The people there were his converts. Paul could have leveraged his authority to ease Timothy's transition at Ephesus, but he didn't. Neither did he encourage Timothy to use his position as the pastor to demand respect. He told Timothy to earn it by his character.

This is a foreign concept in western cultures—even among Christians. We think the goal of life is to care for ourselves and our families well. We promote self and do whatever it takes to protect our best interests so we can get all we can, can all we get, and sit on our can. Then we demand that others recognize our greatness. But Jesus said:

> *If any man will come after me, let him deny himself, and take up his cross, and follow me. For whosoever will save his life shall lose it: and whosoever will lose his life for my sake shall find it.*
>
> **Matthew 16:24–25**

Denying self is repulsive to most people. They don't want to die. They don't want to take up a cross—something you die on—and put God and other people ahead of their own comfort. In Ephesians 6, Paul, speaking under the inspiration of the Holy Spirit, said:

> *Servants, be obedient to them that are your masters according to the flesh, with fear and trembling, in singleness of your heart, as unto Christ; not with eyeservice, as menpleasers; but as the servants of Christ, doing the will of God from the heart.*
>
> **Ephesians 6:5–6**

Those verses make today's readers cringe, even more so when they realize that Paul was speaking into a culture of slavery. And in the midst of this culture, Paul didn't perpetuate the idea that slaves should hate their masters or despise their positions. Instead, he told them to serve *"as unto Christ."* Don't get me wrong; slavery is a horrible practice. It is not God's will. But that was not the point of Paul's statement. Humility was.

Serving others as though you were serving Christ and doing the right thing even when no one is looking—that is the will of God. Most people don't think this way. But when you work only for the promotion and prestige you can gain for yourself, you're not pleasing God. When you goof off anytime the boss isn't looking or habitually come to work late and leave early, you're not honoring Him. When you stretch a ten-minute break into fifteen or take home office supplies thinking no one will notice, you're not serving *"as unto Christ."*

Paul continued in Ephesians 6:8, saying, *"Knowing that whatsoever good thing any man doeth, the same shall he receive of the Lord, whether he be bond or free."* We don't work for the praise and acceptance of people. We don't work to merely pay the bills. We work to honor the Lord. We work so we can be a blessing (Eph. 4:28).

Whether you're a CEO or a janitor, Christ has called you to lay down your life, take up your cross,

❞ Serving others as though you were serving Christ and doing the right thing even when no one is looking—that is the will of God."

and follow Him in serving others—not so you will receive recognition from man, but so God can reward you.

Some might say, "If I had the attitude you're talking about, I'd be run over." That's not true. I've been slandered. People have lied about me. They've accused me of being the "slickest cult since Jim Jones." Once, a person I'd never met came out against me viciously. I knew about the terrible things the person was saying, but I determined not to retaliate, and God worked it out. Eventually we ended up at the same conference. I wasn't a speaker at the meeting but was treated as an honored guest, and God began dealing with that person's heart. Then, in front of 500 people, the person came to the stage, fell at my feet, and asked for forgiveness! There's no way I could have made that happen. But because I left it in God's hands, God defended me.

God can defend you better than you could ever defend yourself! He does not forget the cry of the humble (Ps. 9:12). Scripture says, *"Vengeance is mine; I will repay, saith the Lord"* (Rom. 12:19). Vengeance is God's job. He will right every wrong. Pride will be put in its proper place. But if you take up God's job and defend yourself, you don't leave room for God's judgment. The prophet Isaiah said:

> *The lofty looks of man shall be humbled, and the haughtiness of men shall be bowed down, and the LORD alone shall be exalted in that day. For the day of the LORD of hosts shall be upon every one*

*that is proud and lofty, and upon every one that is
lifted up; and he shall be brought low.*

Isaiah 2:11–12

And King David said: *"He will make your innocence radiate
like the dawn, and the justice of your cause will shine like the noon-
day sun"* (Ps. 37:6, NLT). Be patient, humble yourself, and wait
on the Lord.

This is the way God's kingdom operates. It promotes
humility. Mary, the mother of Jesus, sang, *"He hath put down
the mighty from their seats, and exalted them of low degree"* (Luke
1:52). James, the half-brother of Jesus, wrote, *"Humble yourselves in the sight of the Lord, and he shall lift you up"* (James
4:10). The apostle Peter wrote something similar:

> *Likewise, ye younger, submit yourselves unto the
> elder. Yea, all of you be subject one to another, and be
> clothed with humility: for God resisteth the proud,
> and giveth grace to the humble. Humble yourselves
> therefore under the mighty hand of God, that he
> may exalt you in due time.*

1 Peter 5:5–6

Jesus said, *"But he that is greatest among you shall be your servant. And whosoever shall exalt himself shall be abased; and he
that shall humble himself shall be exalted"* (Matt. 23:11–12). If

you want to experience promotion, if you want God to use you, you have to learn to humble yourself.

I'm not a perfect example of this, but I can truthfully say that I have passed up opportunities to promote myself and to manipulate people into supporting what we're doing around the world. Even though those opportunities looked like they would have "sped up" the growth of the ministry, I choose to humble myself and wait on God. Now God is exalting me, giving me connections and influence I could never have gotten on my own. God is connecting us with movers and shakers in the worlds of entertainment, politics, and business. He's brought top-notch people to help at the ministry and at Charis Bible College. And I now reach more people in one day than I did in years of ministry! It's amazing.

Chapter Five

THE ROOT OF DISOBEDIENCE

The root of disobedience is pride. I know that's a strong statement, and no one likes to hear it, but it's true. Knowing what is right and refusing to do it is sin (James 4:17). And that sin is a direct result of pride.

When Moses and Aaron were in Egypt petitioning Pharaoh for the Israelites' release, the plagues had already begun. Yet Pharaoh refused to relent. He continued to harden his heart and disobey God. Finally, after the seventh plague, Moses and Aaron came to Pharaoh saying, *"Thus saith the* LORD *God of the Hebrews, How long wilt thou refuse to humble thyself before me? let my people go, that they may serve me"* (Ex. 10:3).

Pharaoh's disobedience stemmed from a heart of pride—and so does yours. Any form of disobedience, whether you're addicted to dope or harboring unforgiveness, is pride. It is leaning to your own understanding instead of trusting that God has

> **"Sin doesn't just hurt you; it hurts everyone around you. Your choices are like ever-expanding ripples in a pond."**

your best interests at heart (Prov. 3:5–6). Sin is stupid. Forgive me for being blunt. But sin doesn't just hurt you; it hurts everyone around you. Your choices are like ever-expanding ripples in a pond. They touch everything and everyone within the pond's borders.

I recently called a woman who was a pastor's wife. She and her husband have been supporting us for years. One of her sons was high on booze and meth and killed his dad, her husband, right in front of her. He didn't even remember doing it.

This boy is born-again and Spirit-filled. I'm sure when he finally came to himself, he felt terrible about what he had done, but that didn't change anything. A church is now without a pastor, this woman is without her husband, and this boy is in prison. His choice to do meth and get drunk wasn't just about him. He's hurt many people by his actions.

Your life may seem so miserable that the little bit of time you're numb in sin is a welcome respite, but—I'm saying this in love—life is not all about you. Think of the people who love you. Think of your parents, your children. Pharaoh's choices affected the whole of Egypt. Egyptians who had nothing to do with the Israelite slaves still dealt with the frogs, flies, boils, and hailstorms. Their cattle and children were killed. Their crops were destroyed. Pharaoh's pride crippled the whole of Egypt, not just the palace.

The pain you're experiencing today will not last the whole of your life. Everyone goes through hard times. We all face circumstances that look insurmountable. But there is life ahead of you. There is still good, still joy (Ps. 27:13). I remember when my youngest son was in a season of stupidity. Jamie and I were standing on God's Word for his life, but he was making some really bad decisions. When those decisions finally caught up with him, I remember him saying, "I wasn't hurting anyone but myself." The spirit of slap came all over me! I wanted to scream, "How dumb can you get and still breathe? Look what you did to your mother and me. Look how you affected those around you."

Just as Pharaoh's choices touched all of Egypt, so Nebuchadnezzar's touched the whole of Babylon. His choices even reached down through the generations. In Daniel 5, Nebuchadnezzar's grandson, Belshazzar, had taken over the kingdom. At some point during his reign, he threw a wild party and commanded his servants to use the gold and silver vessels taken from the temple in Jerusalem as serving dishes. He and his guests toasted the gods of gold and silver, brass, iron, stone, and wood with the holy articles in defiance of God and the Jewish people. Suddenly, a hand appeared in the air and wrote "*Mene, Mene, Tekel, Upharsin*" on the wall (Dan. 5:25).

Belshazzar was so spooked, he called for his astrologers and wise men to interpret its meaning. Though he offered great reward, no one could read the writing on the wall. When the queen heard what was happening, she told the king not to worry. She said, *"There is a man in thy kingdom, in whom is the spirit of the holy gods … and he will shew the interpretation"* (Dan. 5:11–12). So, they brought Daniel in. Before Daniel read the writing on the wall and interpreted its meaning to Belshazzar, he told the king to keep his gifts and then recounted the story of his grandfather's struggle with pride:

> *The most high God gave Nebuchadnezzar thy father a kingdom, and majesty, and glory, and honour: and for the majesty that he gave him, all people, nations, and languages, trembled and feared before him: whom he would he slew; and whom he would he kept alive; and whom he would he set up; and whom he would he put down. But when his heart was lifted up, and his mind hardened in pride, he was deposed from his kingly throne, and they took his glory from him: and he was driven from the sons of men; and his heart was made like the beasts, and his dwelling was with the wild asses: they fed him with grass like oxen, and his body was wet with the dew of heaven; till he knew that the most high God ruled in the kingdom of men, and that he appointeth over it whomsoever he will.*

Daniel 5:18–21

Daniel told Belshazzar that God was the source of his grandfather's success. He allowed Nebuchadnezzar to conquer nations and amass wealth and power. But Nebuchadnezzar didn't recognize God as the source of those things. He took the glory of Babylon for himself, and God judged his pride.

I know people struggle with this. They think success is a result of their own efforts, prosperity a

> **We could have been born into a caste system or a country that dictates our level of education, the jobs we can pursue, the property we can own. We are blessed!"**

just reward for the hours they've clocked learning and working and saving. They don't recognize God as their source, but it is God who caused us to live at this time—the most prosperous time in history. He set us in our place. Any one of us could have been born somewhere else in the world. We could have been born into a caste system or a country that dictates our level of education, the jobs we can pursue, the property we can own. We are blessed! God has given us the strength to work. He has given us talents to develop and a functional brain. It wouldn't take much to change that. Just stir the chemicals around a little or throw in an extra chromosome, and we have problems. We need to recognize God's provision and blessing. That's part of humility.

Daniel went on to tell Belshazzar that because his grandfather didn't recognize God, *"his heart was lifted up, and his mind hardened in pride"* (Dan. 5:20). Pride messed with Nebuchadnezzar's mind. It skewed his judgment. It made him spiritually retarded, and it does the same thing today. But Belshazzar did not heed history's warning. Daniel continued, *"And thou . . . O Belshazzar, hast not humbled thine heart, though thou knewest all this"* (Dan. 5:22).

That's amazing. Belshazzar knew in his heart that pride was wrong. He knew God had judged his grandfather's pride, yet he persisted in his own. Maybe Belshazzar thought God wouldn't notice or that God didn't do that kind of thing anymore. Maybe he felt immune to the consequences. I don't know. But I know a lot of people who still live this way. They know in their hearts that disobedience, self-promotion, and pride are wrong. They know God exists and rewards each person according to their deeds, yet they persist in living their own way (Jer. 17:10 and Rev. 22:12). And like Belshazzar, they will eventually reap the consequences.

> **ⁱⁱMaybe Belshazzar thought God wouldn't notice or that God didn't do that kind of thing anymore. Maybe he felt immune to the consequences."**

Daniel interpreted the handwriting on the wall, telling Belshazzar:

> *And this is the writing that was written, MENE, MENE, TEKEL, UPHARSIN. This is the interpretation of the thing: MENE; God hath numbered thy kingdom, and finished it. TEKEL; Thou art weighed in the balances, and art found wanting. PERES;*

*Thy kingdom is divided, and given to the Medes
and Persians.*

Daniel 5:25–28

Babylon was supposed to be impregnable, but that very night, the Medes and Persians invaded and overthrew the kingdom. Belshazzar lost his kingdom because of pride. But did you realize Sodom and Gomorrah also fell because of pride?

*Behold, this was the iniquity of thy sister Sodom,
pride, fulness of bread, and abundance of idleness
was in her and in her daughters, neither did she
strengthen the hand of the poor and needy. And
they were haughty, and committed abomination
before me: therefore I took them away as I saw good.*

Ezekiel 16:49–50

God judged the pride and iniquity of Sodom and Gomorrah with fire and brimstone. He wiped them off the map in a protective measure to ensure their wickedness did not spread like a cancer into the surrounding areas. Homosexuality, and all other forms of sexual perversion, is sin, but the root of that sin is pride.

God created humanity male and female, Adam and Eve. And the Lord God brought Eve to Adam. Scripture says, "*Therefore shall a man leave his father and his mother, and shall cleave unto his wife: and they shall be one flesh*" (Gen. 2:24). Adam and Eve didn't have a mother and father. So, I think it's safe to say that this scripture was not written for their benefit alone. God's definition of marriage is a male leaving his parents' home to "cleave unto" his wife—a female—and create his own family (Mal. 2:15). A man doesn't "cleave unto" a boyfriend (Rom. 1:27). He doesn't "cleave unto" a girlfriend (1 Cor. 6:9-10). He doesn't "cleave unto" a pet or a neighbor's spouse (Lev. 20:15-16 and Ex. 20:14). He "cleaves unto" his wife. No matter what culture says, exalting any opinion above God's is pride. And that pride will eventually lead to sin.

Chapter Six

WHAT GOD REQUIRES

Pride is like a stick—it has two ends. One end is obvious. It shows itself as arrogance and conceit. People operating in this form of pride exaggerate their own successes and pass the blame for their failures, ensuring that others always think well of them. They can't give anyone else credit or celebrate another person's victories. They have to be the center of attention.

The other end of the stick of pride is far more subtle. It presents itself as timidity and low self-esteem—a false humility. People functioning in this form of pride debase and ridicule themselves before others can. They hide in the background, worrying about what others think. They feel unworthy and often struggle to believe. These people know God can heal, deliver, and prosper, but they don't know if He will do those good things for them. They don't feel worthy, but that too is pride.

Pride, in its simplest form, is self-centeredness. It doesn't matter if you're elevating self, hiding self, or debasing self; if your attitudes and actions are focused on self, you're in pride.

Isaiah 3 says:

> *Moreover, the Lord said, Because the daughters of Zion are haughty and walk with outstretched necks and with undisciplined (flirtatious and alluring) eyes, tripping along with mincing and affected gait, and making a tinkling noise with [the anklets on] their feet, therefore the Lord will smite with a scab the crown of the heads of the daughters of Zion [making them bald], and the Lord will cause them to be [taken as captives and to suffer the indignity of being] stripped naked. In that day the Lord will take away the finery of their tinkling anklets, the caps of network, the crescent head ornaments, the pendants, the bracelets or chains, and the spangled face veils and scarfs, the headbands, the short ankle chains [attached from one foot to the other to insure a measured gait], the sashes, the perfume boxes, the amulets or charms [suspended from the ears or neck], the signet rings and nose rings, the festal robes, the cloaks, the stoles and shawls, and the handbags, the hand mirrors, the fine linen [undergarments], the turbans, and the [whole body-enveloping] veils.*
>
> **Isaiah 3:16–23, AMPC**

This is probably not a passage of Scripture highlighted in your Bible, but it is very descriptive of our day and age. Reading it is like looking through a fashion magazine or watching a television commercial. It talks about all the things being promoted and lauded by the trendsetters of our day—clothing, posture, jewelry, makeup, hairdos, and perfume. Though these verses are directed at women, they do not apply only to women. They apply to every person wasting their lives on pride, self-promotion, and outward appearance. And what are the results of this kind of lifestyle? Notice what the next verse in Isaiah says:

> *And it shall come to pass that instead of the sweet odor of spices there shall be the stench of rottenness; and instead of a girdle, a rope; and instead of well-set hair, baldness; and instead of a rich robe, a girding of sackcloth; and searing [of captives by the scorching heat] instead of beauty.*
>
> **Isaiah 3:24, AMPC**

It all disappears. Peter echoed this passage in 1 Peter. He said, *"Whose adorning let it not be that outward adorning of plaiting the hair, and of wearing of gold, or of putting on of apparel; but let it be the hidden man of the heart, in that which is not corruptible, even the ornament of a meek and quiet spirit, which is in the sight of God of great price"* (1 Pet. 3:3–4).

Now, there is balance to this. These verses are not saying it's wrong to wear nice clothes or fix your hair or wear jewelry. I know there are religious sects that have taken this principle to an extreme, not allowing women to cut their hair or wear jewelry or pants. I've actually known naturally beautiful people who were made to wear makeup to cover up their rosy cheeks and lips. That's weird. If this verse were really forbidding the wearing of gold or braiding of hair, then it would also be forbidding the wearing of clothes. People who criticize others with this verse are doing exactly what this verse says not to do—they are looking at only outward appearances.

❝Beauty is only skin deep. It doesn't last long. But a godly and humble attitude of heart is attractive at any age.❞

These verses are not giving us a list of rules to follow. There's plenty of room in God's grace for variance in dress and grooming habits. But spending more time on apparel, makeup, and hairdos than on seeking the Lord is out of balance. First Peter says our *"adorning"* should not be based on outward appearance but on *"the hidden man of the heart."* Beauty is only skin deep. It doesn't last long. But a godly and humble attitude of heart is attractive at any age.

Jeremiah 10:23 says, *"O LORD, I know that the way of man is not in himself: it is not in man that walketh to direct his steps."* We have a choice. We can choose to direct our own steps, or we can choose to step off the throne of our lives and put God there. Humility is turning our lives over to God, saying, "God,

You're the source. I'm not smart enough to run my own life. I need You." Humility is the condition of our hearts submitted to God.

In 1 Peter 5:7, we are told to cast all our cares upon the Lord because He cares for us. If you feel burdened by the weight of family relationships, work demands, or personal obligations, you're not casting your care on the Lord. If you're staying awake at night worried about a to-do list, you haven't humbled yourself. You can't fix everything. You can only do what God tells you to do; then you must leave the rest in His hands (1 Cor. 3:7). Trust that God will be your *"ever-present help"* (Ps. 46:1, GW).

When my youngest son was three years old, God spoke this truth to my heart in a very practical way. My son and I were coming out of a public restroom whose door sat heavily on a spring-loaded hinge. It was difficult to open. My son grabbed the knob and pulled for all he was worth, but he couldn't make the door budge. He tried getting more leverage by planting his foot on the door, but that was counterproductive. He turned to me with his hands still wrapped around the knob, silently pleading for help. "Peter," I told him, "until you let go, I can't open the door. I'll hurt your hands." Immediately the Lord spoke to my heart. "Andrew, until you let go of your problems, I can't help without hurting you either."

I've remembered those words over the years, especially during this building phase in Woodland Park. At the time of this writing, we've spent over $90 million building a first-class

Bible college campus in the mountains of Colorado. But we're just getting started. There are hundreds of millions of dollars' worth of vision in my heart! I'm humbled and thankful for what God has done in the last decade through Andrew Wommack Ministries and Charis, but I know if He'd asked me to do these things eleven years ago, I'd have panicked. I remember when the ministry struggled to pay bills of $2,000, and I couldn't sleep at night. Thank God I've grown since then! I now understand that it's not my responsibility to produce the things God's placed in my heart. My job is to respond in faith to His ability, knowing that where He guides, He is responsible to provide. Today the ministry requires thousands of dollars every hour to meet its obligations. That's a lot of money, money I don't personally have. But I'm able to sleep at night. I've learned to cast my care on the Lord. That's humility.

Relationship with God is not supposed to be complicated. We aren't required to memorize a bunch of rules or prove our devotion to God through rituals and sacrifice. Jesus fulfilled the Law's requirements (Matt. 5:17). All God asks of us is summed up in the book of Micah:

> *He hath shewed thee, O man, what is good; and what doth the LORD require of thee, but to do justly, and to love mercy, and to walk humbly with thy God?*

Micah 6:8

Do justly, love mercy, and walk humbly with God. Not many people do that today—mainly because it's not taught. Romans 10:17 says that *"faith cometh by hearing, and hearing by the word of God."* We can't have faith or believe for something we've never heard. If we don't understand that humility releases the grace of God, we won't experience His grace. If we don't know the danger and subtleties of pride, we can't resist it. That's why I'm trying to overwhelm you with scriptural evidence for humility. I want to produce faith in you—faith to resist pride and recognize true humility. True humility is not focused on self. It has surrendered to God, putting His will and others' well-being ahead of its own.

> *"My job is to respond in faith to His ability, knowing that where He guides, He is responsible to provide."*

Chapter Seven

THE RESPONSE OF HUMILITY

Our society doesn't understand humility. Even Christians have become self-centered, self-promoting, and self-reliant. They are contentious, demanding, and critical. They have not died to self (Matt. 16:24). They crave recognition. They exalt their own opinions and experiences above God's Word. Instead of looking unto Jesus (Heb. 12:2), most people look at themselves, and they struggle to believe. Because they have not cast their care upon the Lord (1 Pet. 5:7), they become weary and give up their faith. Pride traps them. It hinders them from experiencing the full benefits of God's grace.

Jesus once said, *"Out of the abundance of the heart the mouth speaketh"* (Matt. 12:34). If your heart is full of pride, your words will show it, for *"by thy words thou shalt be justified, and by thy words thou shalt be condemned"* (Matt. 12:37).

Before the prophet Samuel was born, his mother was barren. In those days, barren women were thought to be cursed. Without children, a woman couldn't fulfill her societal role, nor would she have anyone to care for her in old age. Samuel's mother, Hannah, was heartbroken over her barrenness and prayed fervently for a child. She even vowed that if God would open her womb, she would give her first child back to Him. Once when she and her husband, Elkanah, went to Shiloh to worship, the priest saw her praying. He assumed she was drunk and started to rebuke her. Hannah told him of her heartbreak, and the priest blessed her instead (1 Sam. 1).

Hannah returned home with her husband and, over the course of time, conceived Samuel. When she brought Samuel before the Lord to fulfill her vow, she prayed, *"My heart rejoiceth in the LORD . . . There is none holy as the LORD: for there is none beside thee: neither is there any rock like our God"* (1 Sam. 2:1-2). She went on, saying:

> *Talk no more so exceeding proudly; let not arrogancy come out of your mouth: for the LORD is a God of knowledge, and by him actions are weighed.*
>
> **1 Samuel 2:3**

God heard the proud words and criticism Hannah endured as a barren woman—even from her own household—and He did not remain silent. He vindicated Hannah by giving her sons and daughters (1 Sam. 2:21). He also chastised Peninnah,

Elkanah's other wife and Hannah's loudest critic, for her treatment of Hannah (1 Sam. 2:5). Brothers and sisters, there's a lot of proud talk today—even among Christians—and it is not wise.

> *Ye fools, when will ye be wise? He that planted the ear, shall he not hear? he that formed the eye, shall he not see? He that chastiseth the heathen, shall not he correct? he that teacheth man knowledge, shall not he know? The LORD knoweth the thoughts of man, that they are vanity.*
>
> **Psalm 94:8b–11**

Hebrews reminds us:

> *For we know him that hath said, Vengeance belongeth unto me, I will recompense, saith the Lord. And again, The Lord shall judge his people.*
>
> **Hebrews 10:30**

The Lord is gracious (Ps. 145:8). He does not treat us as our sins deserve (Ps. 103:10) but gives us time to repent, time to acknowledge that pride (which is the root of anger, criticism, and

❞Brothers and sisters, there's a lot of proud talk today—even among Christians—and it is not wise."

every other sin) does not produce righteousness (James 1:20). No matter what experience says, the end does not justify the means. God gives us time to acknowledge His grace and humble ourselves (2 Pet. 3:9). But a day will come when He *"shall judge his people."*

Job discovered this truth thousands of years ago. The Bible calls Job, a pre-covenant follower of God, *"the greatest of all the men of the east"* (Job 1:3). He was prosperous and healthy. He feared God and shunned evil. But in one day, Job lost everything he had. His children were killed. His wealth was taken. Many of his servants lost their lives. Then, before he had time to recover, he was struck with painful boils.

When his friends heard of Job's distress, they came to "comfort" him. For seven days they sat in the dirt and grieved. No one said a word. When Job finally opened his mouth, hurt and bitterness spewed forth. He cursed the day he was born. He wished for death (Job 3). It wasn't until Job's friends spoke up that things changed. "You're angry and bitter without cause," they said. "Bad things don't happen to good people. Your own sin has brought this calamity upon you."

"If I have sinned," Job replied, "show me what I've done wrong. I don't know why this is happening to me, but I know I'm innocent."

Much of the book of Job is this back-and-forth conversation between Job and his friends. But their counsel did not help him; it only caused more grief. At some point during their conversation, Job began to question God. There was a subtle shift from "I don't know why this is happening to me" to "This is not fair. God is unjust. There is no benefit to serving Him" (Job 34:9). His friends finally *"ceased to answer Job, because he was righteous in his own eyes"* (Job 32:1).

After everything got quiet, God spoke. But He did not explain Himself to Job. He did not answer Job's questions. He only addressed Job's folly. For four chapters—Job 38 through 41—the Lord reminded Job of who He is (and of who Job was). God sarcastically asked, "Where were you when I formed the earth? Did you give the horse its strength? Do you shut the sea behind its doors? Can you bring forth the constellations in their seasons? Do you know where light resides? Have you visited the storehouses of snow? Does the eagle soar at your command? Can you pull in the leviathan with a fishhook? Are you the one who gives man wisdom and understanding?"

> *But of course you know all this! For you were born before it was all created, and you are so very experienced!*
>
> **Job 38:21, NLT**

God continued, "If you're righteousness truly exceeds that of my own, then do what I do":

Deck thyself now with majesty and excellency; and array thyself with glory and beauty. Cast abroad the rage of thy wrath: and behold every one that is proud, and abase him. Look on every one that is proud, and bring him low; and tread down the wicked in their place.

Job 40:10–12

God abases pride, but He also exalts the humble (1 Pet. 5:6). Notice Job's response to God:

I know that thou canst do every thing, and that no thought can be withholden from thee. Who is he that hideth counsel without knowledge? therefore have I uttered that I understood not; things too wonderful for me, which I knew not. . . . I have heard of thee by the hearing of the ear: but now mine eye seeth thee. Wherefore I abhor myself, and repent in dust and ashes.

Job 42:2–3 and 5–6

Job humbled himself. He repented, and God restored everything Satan stole from him. Repentance and humility are the proper response to God's correction. As a matter of fact, in Scripture, every time a person saw the glory of God, humility was the result. When Isaiah saw the Lord, he repented: *"Woe is me! for I am undone; because I am a man of unclean lips, and I dwell in the midst of a people of unclean lips: for mine eyes have seen the King, the LORD of hosts*" (Is. 6:5). When God spoke to Abram, he fell on his face (Gen. 17:3). When the Lord spoke to Moses out of the burning bush, Moses hid his face because he was afraid to look upon Him (Ex. 3:5–6). When the angel appeared before Joshua, he bowed to the ground in reverence (Josh. 5:14).

Intimacy with God is impossible outside true humility.

> *Though the Lord be high, yet hath he respect unto the lowly: but the proud he knoweth afar off.*
>
> **Psalm 138:6**

If we could ever catch a glimpse of God's glory—His grace—we would humble ourselves. We would lose all arrogance and pride.

I've heard many people say things like, "When I get to heaven I'm going to ask God why He let this or that happen. Why didn't He intervene in this situation?" But in heaven, no one will be standing in line to ask God questions, trying to discover the reason behind every suffering. When

❝When we finally see God for who He really is, we will fall on our faces in humility and be saying, 'Praise God I didn't ask that stupid question.'"

we finally see God for who He really is, we will fall on our faces in humility and be saying, "Praise God I didn't ask that stupid question."

You know, I've never seen God with my physical eyes. But I had an experience with the Lord on March 23, 1968, that changed my life. My small group was meeting for prayer as usual, and though I didn't see anything, I knew God was in that place. In a moment, I felt God's love. I experienced His holiness. I finally understood who God was, and I fell on my face in repentance. Don't get me wrong. I believe I was saved before that moment, and I believe I would have gone to heaven. But that moment of humility changed the trajectory of my life. It opened the door for me to experience real relationship with God.

Chapter Eight

THE FACE
OF HUMILITY

Most people think humility is weakness or timidity. Jesus described Himself as *"meek and lowly in heart"* (Matt. 11:29), but He wasn't weak or timid. He was bold! He didn't fear the religious leaders of His day. He called them vipers and whitewashed tombs (Matt. 12:34 and 23:27). He even called Herod—the puppet-king of Israel—a fox (Luke 13:32). Two different times during His ministry, Jesus drove people out of the temple and turned over the money changers' tables in righteous indignation (Matt. 21:12 and John 2:15).

Even Moses acted in humility when he burned the golden calf his brother made. He ground its ashes into powder, threw the ashes on the water, and made the Israelites drink it (Ex. 32:19-20). Numbers describes Moses as the meekest man on the face of the earth (Num. 12:3). But did you realize Moses wrote the book of Numbers? Under the inspiration of the Holy

Spirit, Moses called himself the meekest, or most humble, man on the face of the earth.

Most people would think if you are truly humble, you wouldn't know it or certainly wouldn't admit it as Moses did. Therefore, we need to redefine humility.

Religion has warped our perception of true humility. It has taught that humility is weakness or low self-esteem, an attitude of self-abasement and timidity. Religious humility says, "I am nothing; I can do nothing." But if humility were what the church has portrayed for decades, a truly humble person would never know they were humble. I heard a story about a man who was honored by his church as being its most humble member. The church got together and made him a huge button that said "Humble" and presented it to him one day during service. But when they presented the button to him, he didn't refuse their gift or deflect their praise, so they took the button back. They said if he was truly humble, he wouldn't have accepted their praise.

A woman in the church where I grew up expressed this sentiment each time she got up to sing. She would say, "The Lord says to make a joyful noise, so that's what I'm going to do today. You all pray for me. I know I don't have a great voice, but I'm going to make a joyful noise." Then she'd let loose a trained operatic voice that shook the rafters! She wasn't humble; she was fishing for a compliment. It was all a religious con! She only debased herself in the hopes that someone else would praise her. I bet she wouldn't have responded well if I'd met her outside church and said, "You're right, sister. You can't sing!"

Humility doesn't exalt self. It doesn't abase self either. True humility doesn't have an opinion of self. It only seeks to glorify God. If God has given you a great voice or a talent for business, true

> **" True humility doesn't have an opinion of self. It only seeks to glorify God."**

humility will honor that gift. It won't deny what God has given. Nor will it deny what God does through His gift. Paul said:

> *For who maketh thee to differ from another? and what hast thou that thou didst not receive? now if thou didst receive it, why dost thou glory, as if thou hadst not received it?*

> **1 Corinthians 4:7**

Everything you have comes from God. Humility acknowledges this. God exalts those who are humble (James 4:10 and 1 Pet. 5:6), and those who are truly humble will let Him. The proud won't. The proud will be too concerned about what others might think. They will try to deflect the honor by debasing themselves. That's not humility. When Moses said he was the meekest man on the face of the earth, that was an accurate assessment. God inspired him to write it. It would have been prideful to disagree with God. It would have been prideful to say, "God, I can't write that! What would people think?"

Brothers and sisters, I say these things with conviction because, in the natural, I am an introvert. As a young man, I couldn't look a person in the face and talk to them. I was fine around friends and family, but strangers petrified me. One time a man greeted me on the street; he was two blocks away and I was sitting in my car before I worked up the strength to respond! I was so timid and focused on self. I always struggled with people's names. Every time I was introduced to someone new, my attention would be focused on looking good and answering correctly and I wouldn't even hear their name! Thankfully, when I first started out in ministry, a man approached me and said, "You've got some really good things to say. If you ever became more concerned about the people you're ministering to than you are about yourself and what they think of you, you could be a blessing." His words were like a dagger to the heart, but they were true. My timidity wasn't a result of my personality. It was self-centeredness and pride. I was worried that I would say something wrong or make a fool of myself.

This is the case with many people. Though God has delivered them from destructive lifestyles and they have a great testimony, they don't share it because they're afraid. They're worried they won't say or do something "correctly." That's pride. Today, by the grace of God, I speak to hundreds of students every week, thousands of people at each meeting, and even more by television, but I'm still not an eloquent speaker. As a matter of fact, if I were God, I wouldn't have chosen me. I would have chosen a better communicator, someone who doesn't sound like Gomer Pyle. But God did choose me (1 Cor. 1:27), and because I chose to humble myself, He's using me to reach millions.

> *For I say, through the grace given unto me, to every man that is among you, not to think of himself more highly than he ought to think; but to think soberly, according as God hath dealt to every man the measure of faith.*

Romans 12:3

We're not supposed to think too highly or too lowly of ourselves. We're just supposed to think soberly. Paul said, *"Let nothing be done through strife or vainglory; but in lowliness of mind let each esteem other better than themselves"* (Phil. 2:3). The New International Version says, *"In humility value others above yourselves."*

That doesn't mean others are better than you are. It means you place the proper value on each person. Every person on this planet was created in God's image. Each one is designed by God for a specific purpose. Our differences don't make us less valuable; they make us more valuable. There's no one else on the planet exactly like you, and there's nothing wrong with recognizing the talents and abilities God has given you. There's nothing wrong with acknowledging what God has accomplished through your life. Just make sure you're giving God the glory and honoring what God is doing in and through others.

"Our differences don't make us less valuable; they make us more valuable. There's no one else on the planet exactly like you, and there's nothing wrong with recognizing the talents and abilities God has given you."

Jesus's story in Luke 18 about the Pharisee and the publican illustrates how difficult it is for proud people to honor others and even God. Pharisees were members of the Jewish ruling council. They were experts in Jewish law, and they showed their piety through the clothes they wore, the things they ate, and the way they prayed. A publican, though Jewish, worked for the Roman government collecting taxes. Publicans were viewed as traitors and often overcharged their fellow Jews, keeping the excess for themselves. In Jesus's story, a publican and a Pharisee went to the temple to pray.

> *The Pharisee stood and prayed thus with himself, God, I thank thee, that I am not as other men are, extortioners, unjust, adulterers, or even as this publican. I fast twice in the week, I give tithes of all that I possess.*

> ### Luke 18:11–12

In another place, Jesus told his disciples not to pray like the hypocrites who stand in the temple or on the street corners, praying to be seen of men (Matt. 6:5). Notice how Jesus described the Pharisee in Luke 18. He said the Pharisee *"prayed with himself."* He wasn't communicating or connecting with God. He was praying to be seen. He was praying in pride. The majority of his prayer was a justification of self, an exalting of his good deeds in the hopes that God would hear him. Many people pray like this. Their prayers don't connect with God or change anything. They're just hot air used to impress people or meet some religious quota.

> **❝ God doesn't owe us anything. We may be holier than the person in the next pew, but who wants to be the best sinner who ever went to hell?"**

Religious posturing—the use of good deeds, Bible reading, the paying of tithes, church attendance, or any other "good work" to bribe God into answering prayer or moving on our behalf—is pride. God doesn't owe us anything. We may be holier than the person in the next pew, but who wants to be the best sinner who ever went to hell? (Compare Romans 3:23 with Romans 6:23.) Yet people ask, "Why hasn't God healed me? I pray. I go to church. I pay my tithes. I've done this and this and that." The answer is in the question. We can't approach God based on our own holiness or goodness. We've all fallen short of His glory (Rom. 3:23). We can't earn healing or any of God's blessings. We have to approach God like the publican did:

And the publican, standing afar off, would not lift up so much as his eyes unto heaven, but smote upon his breast, saying, God be merciful to me a sinner.

Luke 18:13

The publican wasn't prideful. He didn't try to justify himself in the sight of God. He didn't talk about all his good deeds. He humbled himself, not even lifting his eyes to heaven, and Jesus said that this man—the humble publican—went home justified (Luke 18:14).

When we humble ourselves and stand before God trusting in His grace and mercy, He hears us. And 1 John says that if we know He hears us, we know we have whatever we've asked of Him (1 John 5:14-15).

Chapter Nine

THE RESULTS
OF HUMILITY

King Hezekiah reigned over Judah during the life of the prophet Isaiah. Second Chronicles 29:2 says he *"did that which was right in the sight of the LORD."* But at some point during his reign, King Hezekiah got into pride (2 Chr. 32:25). When the Babylonians heard how the Lord had miraculously healed Hezekiah, they came to see him. Instead of giving glory to God for all He had done to heal him and prosper the kingdom, Hezekiah showed off everything in his storehouses (2 Kings 20:12–13). Isaiah confronted the king about his error, saying, *"Behold, the days come, that all that is in thine house, and that which thy fathers have laid up in store unto this day, shall be carried into Babylon: nothing shall be left, saith the LORD"* (2 Kings 20:17, see Is. 39:5–6). Then Hezekiah humbled himself:

> *Then Hezekiah repented of the pride of his heart,*
> *as did the people of Jerusalem; therefore the LORD's*

> *wrath did not come on them during the days of Hezekiah.*

2 Chronicles 32:26, NIV

Because he humbled himself, God granted Hezekiah and his kingdom an extension of peace. During this time, Hezekiah had a son named Manasseh. Manasseh became king when he was only twelve years old. The Bible says he *"did that which was evil in the sight of the LORD"* (2 Chr. 33:2). He rebuilt the pagan shrines his father had torn down. He constructed altars of Baal and sacrificed his own children on them, set up idols in the temple, worshiped the stars, and practiced sorcery (2 Kings 21:2–6). Second Kings 21:9 says he led Judah to do more evil than the pagan nations God drove out before the Israelites. Though the Lord warned Manasseh of the consequences of his pride, he would not listen. So, Assyria invaded the kingdom of Judah and carried Manasseh into captivity. But during his captivity, he turned to God:

> *And when he* [Manasseh] *was in affliction, he besought the LORD his God, and humbled himself greatly before the God of his fathers, and prayed unto him: and he was intreated of him, and heard his supplication, and brought him again to Jerusalem into his kingdom. Then Manasseh knew that the LORD he was God.*

2 Chronicles 33:12–13

Manasseh humbled himself and repented. And God brought him back to Jerusalem, reinstating him as king. Manasseh reigned a total of fifty-five years, becoming the longest reigning king in Israel's history. After humbling himself, Manasseh removed the idols and altars he had built to false gods, and he restored the altar of the Lord. The Bible says, *"The rest of the acts of Manasseh, and his prayer unto his God . . . and all his sins . . . before he was humbled: behold, they are written among the sayings of the seers"* (2 Chr. 33:18–19).

Even though Manasseh spent most of his life doing evil in the sight of the Lord, God honored him when he humbled himself, and the end of his days was good.

Manasseh's son Amon took the throne after him. Amon followed his father's earlier evil example, but he refused to humble himself and was assassinated (2 Chr. 33:22–24).

Amon's son Josiah inherited the throne at eight years old (2 Chr. 34:1). When Josiah turned sixteen, he began to seek the Lord. Four years later, he began to purge Judah of idol worship, and he commanded that the temple be repaired.

During the temple repair process, a priest found the Book of the Law of Moses, and it was read to the king. When Josiah heard God's standards—probably for the

❝ Even though Manasseh spent most of his life doing evil in the sight of the Lord, God honored him when he humbled himself, and the end of his days was good.❞

first time in his life—and realized how Judah had sinned, he humbled himself, and the Lord saw his heart. When he inquired of the Lord what he and the people should do, the prophetess Huldah prophesied good for King Josiah, but judgment for the kingdom of Judah:

> *Thus saith the LORD God of Israel, Tell ye the man that sent you to me, Thus saith the LORD, Behold, I will bring evil upon this place, and upon the inhabitants thereof, even all the curses that are written in the book which they have read before the king of Judah: because they have forsaken me, and have burned incense unto other gods, that they might provoke me to anger with all the works of their hands; therefore my wrath shall be poured out upon this place, and shall not be quenched. And **as for the king of Judah**, who sent you to enquire of the LORD, so shall ye say unto him, Thus saith the LORD God of Israel concerning the words which thou hast heard; **because thine heart was tender, and thou didst humble thyself before God,** when thou heardest his words against this place, and against the inhabitants thereof, **and humbledst thyself before me**, and didst rend thy clothes, and weep before me; I have even heard thee also, saith the LORD. Behold, I will gather thee to thy fathers, and **thou shalt be gathered to thy grave in peace, neither shall thine eyes see all the evil that I will***

bring upon this place, and upon the inhabitants of the same.

2 Chronicles 34:23–28

Notice what God said to Josiah: "Because you have humbled yourself, I will grant you peace. Your eyes will not see the judgment of this people's pride." Josiah's humility not only postponed God's judgment, sparing the people, but it also brought about a great revival. Many people today pray for revival, but they haven't humbled themselves (2 Chr. 7:14). They are still doing their own thing, still depending on and promoting themselves. They are prideful, and their pride limits what God can do in their lives.

People often approach me wanting information about Charis Bible College. They say they want to attend, but they can't figure out how to make it work. They worry about finances, family relationships, work opportunities, housing, and a host of other things. One couple actually told me they'd come to Colorado in a heartbeat, but they had two dogs to think of. "We have dogs in Colorado," I said.

Another guy told me, "I wish I could come, but I sleep under a bridge."

"We have bridges in Colorado," I told him.

I know that sounds funny, but no excuse justifies disobedience. If God told you to do something, do it. That's humility. If you have to debate with God, if it takes you a week, a month, a year to submit to His instructions, you're proud. You're thinking you know more than God. You are exalting your own opinion above His. Humility submits. It acknowledges that there is only one God, and you're not Him.

When the Lord touched my life on March 23, 1968, and I stepped off the throne, I made a decision to follow Him wherever He led and do whatever He said, regardless of the consequences. The first thing God told me was to quit school. I was in my first year of college, and it was during the Vietnam War. The US military was actively drafting men for the conflict, but I had a student deferment. Obeying God meant I would lose that deferment and be drafted. It meant I could be shipped to Vietnam and possibly die. But I obeyed.

Looking back, being drafted was one of the best things that could've happened to me. It separated me from the religious environment where I was raised. Not that my environment was bad—I got saved there. But that separation forced me into the Word of God. It forced me to trust God. For thirteen months, I spent up to fifteen hours a day studying the Bible. I was introduced to the Holy Spirit, the believer's authority, faith and miracles, and so much more—things I'd never been taught in church.

> **❪❪ No excuse justifies disobedience. If God told you to do something, do it. That's humility."**

By the grace of God, I survived Vietnam. But when I came back, jobs were scarce. I was a college dropout, and the chances of succeeding without a college degree looked slim. But God took care of me. My first job was editing and delivering reel-to-reel videos for the public school system. Before long, the district supervisor offered me a permanent job with retirement benefits. My mother thought it was a wonderful opportunity and encouraged me to take the job, but I had to give them a five-year commitment. I knew God had called me to the ministry, and I felt I needed to be able to leave whenever and go wherever God directed, so I turned it down. Everyone thought I was crazy.

Years later, Jamie and I began pastoring a little church in Childress, Texas. It grew to nearly fifty people, and for the first time in our married life, it looked like we were going to survive. We were eating regularly, and things were working out. But then God called us to Pritchett, Colorado. Pritchett may not have been the end of the world, but you could certainly see it from there! Only 144 people lived in the whole town. It looked like a decisive step backward, but Pritchett ended up being a launching pad for our ministry. We saw a man raised from the dead there. Our first partners came from there, and we started on radio there. It was awesome.

About that time, God told me to give away all my ministry materials. When I started doing that, I didn't know another person on the planet who was or ever had given their stuff away. Multiple people told me I would kill the ministry by doing that, but I obeyed. And today we are prospering! In 2018, over 68.2 million came into the ministry—and many of the people who contact the ministry or ask for products don't give a thing! We've given away millions and millions of tapes, books, CDs, DVDs, and digital downloads. It doesn't make sense, but God honored my humble obedience.

Our puny logic cannot begin to comprehend the ways of God. We don't see things as He does. Isaiah 55:9 says:

> *For as the heavens are higher than the earth, so are my ways higher than your ways, and my thoughts than your thoughts.*

We can't look into eternity and know how our actions will affect the future, but He can. If we would just humble ourselves and trust that His plans for us are beyond anything we could hope or imagine, I guarantee things would work out (Jer. 29:11). Life would be good. God created each one of us, and He knows what will satisfy us. He knows how to care for us better than we can care for ourselves!

It doesn't make sense, but God honored my humble obedience."

Chapter Ten

HUMILITY OBEYS

It's important to develop a godly perspective on humility because there are ditches on either side of this road. On one side is arrogance—thinking you're a self-made man or woman, taking credit for everything that's happening in your life. On the other is a religious con called false humility—thinking you'll never accomplish anything of significance for God and devaluing your life. Both attitudes are wrong; both are pride.

True humility does not promote or debase self. It agrees with God and submits to the authority of His Word. If the Word says you are the righteousness of God and can do all things through Christ who strengthens you (2 Cor. 5:21 and Phil. 4:13), it would be pride to disagree. If the Word says you can lay hands on the sick and they'll recover (Mark 16:18), exalting your religious opinion over God's opinion is arrogance.

I've said many times that my natural tendency is timidity. Without Christ, I'm an introvert. I can't talk to people or lead them. But with Christ, my whole life is spent doing what I can't do in the natural. Mark 16:17–18 says:

> *And these signs shall follow them that believe; In my name shall they cast out devils; they shall speak with new tongues; they shall take up serpents; and if they drink any deadly thing, it shall not hurt them; they shall lay hands on the sick, and they shall recover.*

I am a believer, so it's humility for me to declare that God has anointed me to heal the sick, speak in tongues, and cast out devils. It is humility to know that God is with me and that whatever I set my hand to prospers (Deut. 28:8). It is humility to say that God will supply all my needs and that I can build Charis Bible College (Phil. 4:19). It's humility for me to be bold and proclaim the Word of God over my life. I know I can't do any of these things in myself, but in Christ, I can do everything He calls me to do (Phil. 4:13). That's humility.

But the majority of people don't let the Bible get in the way of what they believe. They refuse to submit to its authority, following the whim of popular opinion instead. This is especially true during election years in the United States. Good people, even Christians, base their vote on what media personalities say instead of what the Bible says.

" True humility does not promote or debase self. It agrees with God and submits to the authority of His Word."

They selfishly vote for those who promise them "free" college or "free" health care. A few years ago, I heard that a group of people were promised free cell phones if they would register to vote for a certain party platform. Of course, I don't know if that's true, but it certainly sounds like human nature. Humility doesn't do that. It doesn't exalt self at the expense of others. Humility obeys God.

The book of Acts calls David a man after God's own heart (Acts 13:22), but David was a sinner. Not just any sinner; he was a royal sinner! David sinned big time, committing adultery with Bathsheba and murdering her husband to cover it up (2 Sam. 11). This happened at a time when David should have been on the battlefield.

When David was king, nations warred when the weather was conducive for battle. And although David still had territories to win to accomplish God's will, he got comfortable. He had reached a measure of success, and it was no longer required of him to personally appear at each battle. Enough trustworthy people had rallied around him that David could send Joab, his military commander, to fight instead.

And it came to pass in an eveningtide, that David arose from off his bed, and walked upon the roof of the king's house: and from the roof he saw a woman

washing herself; and the woman was very beauti-
ful to look upon.

2 Samuel 11:2

Young David would have never considered this course of action. Remember when he was running from Saul? David had killed Goliath, rousing Saul's jealousy, and was hiding in caves and among the enemy nations of Israel. As Saul pursued David, Saul stopped to relieve himself in a cave where David was hiding. In that moment, David could have killed Saul and taken the throne, but he didn't. He was humble. He refused to usurp authority or do something independent of God (1 Sam. 24).

But during this season of success, David was not out doing what he was anointed to do. He was home, bored. He was a successful and respected king. His treasuries were full. He'd reached his goals, and his success went to his head. David no longer had to depend upon God. He could take what he wanted, and he wanted Bathsheba.

You wouldn't think such a prideful man could be called "a man after God's own heart." But when the prophet Nathan confronted David about his sin and pride, David did the right thing. He humbled himself (2 Sam. 12).

Contrast that with the way Saul responded to the Lord's rebuke (1 Sam. 13). In the second year of Saul's reign, when Saul went out to fight the Philistines, he was grossly outnumbered.

The people with him were terrified and fled, but Saul waited to inquire of the Lord. He waited for seven days (the time set by the prophet Samuel), and when he didn't see Samuel coming, Saul unlawfully offered the sacrifice. As he was finishing, Samuel appeared.

> *And Samuel said to Saul, Thou hast done foolishly: thou hast not kept the commandment of the LORD thy God, which he commanded thee: for now would the LORD have established thy kingdom upon Israel for ever. But now thy kingdom shall not continue: the LORD hath sought him a man after his own heart, and the LORD hath commanded him to be captain over his people, because thou hast not kept that which the LORD commanded thee.*

1 Samuel 13:13–14

Both David and Saul sinned, but by comparison, Saul's sin doesn't seem as grievous. Saul didn't commit adultery. He didn't try to cover his sin by murdering his mistress's husband. Yet when Saul was confronted with his sin, he refused to humble himself. Then, in 1 Samuel 15, Samuel gave Saul instructions to wipe out the Amalekites and destroy everything, including the women, children, and animals. But Saul did not obey the Lord. He spared Agag, the king, and kept the best of the animals for himself. Again, when Samuel confronted Saul, Saul replied, "I did what the Lord commanded. I destroyed the

Amalekites and brought back King Agag as proof. It was the people who took the spoil and spared the best of the sheep and oxen to sacrifice to the Lord" (1 Sam. 15:20–21).

Instead of humbling himself, Saul argued with the prophet and made excuses for his behavior. And it cost him the kingdom. Samuel said:

> *When thou wast little in thine own sight, wast thou not made the head of the tribes of Israel, and the LORD anointed thee king over Israel? . . . And Samuel said, Hath the LORD as great delight in burnt offerings and sacrifices, as in obeying the voice of the LORD? Behold, to obey is better than sacrifice, and to hearken than the fat of rams.*

1 Samuel 15:17 and 22

When Samuel anointed Saul as the first king over Israel, he went through an elaborate presentation to show the way God chooses leaders. He had all the tribes of Israel pass by him, and then he chose the smallest tribe, Benjamin. Then he had all the leaders of the families of Benjamin pass by, and he chose the least family, Kish (1 Sam. 9:21). Finally Saul was chosen. But Saul could not be found. He was hiding in a basket. And though Saul was a handsome man and taller than anyone else in the kingdom, the Lord did not choose him for that reason (1 Sam. 16:7). He chose Saul and exalted him because Saul was humble. But because Saul refused to obey the Lord or humble himself when his sin was brought to light, the Lord *"rejected* [him] *from being king"* (1 Sam. 15:23).

After delivering those heavy words, Samuel tried to walk away. Saul fell to the ground, grabbing hold of the prophet's robe and begged, *"I have sinned: yet honour me now, I pray thee, before the elders of my people, and before Israel, and turn again with me, that I may worship the LORD thy God"* (1 Sam. 15:30).

Saul had just lost God's favor, but all he cared about was the people's approval! That is pride.

> *For thus saith the high and lofty One that inhabiteth eternity, whose name is Holy; I dwell in the high and holy place, with him also that is of a contrite and humble spirit, to revive the spirit of the humble, and to revive the heart of the contrite ones.*
>
> **Isaiah 57:15**

God, the high and lofty One, dwells with the humble. He chooses to fellowship with them. That's amazing. Humility attracts God, and humility obeys.

You may be thinking, *But Andrew, I thought grace was unconditional. Are you saying that I have to do something to experience God's grace and favor in my life?* No, I'm not saying that. Grace *is* unconditional. It's not based on your performance. David sinned grievously, but he humbled himself and received the grace of God. So, you could say that while grace is unconditional, it is proportional to your humility. You don't have to be perfect. But be quick to repent. Humble yourself and fess up when you mess up. James 4:6 says, *"God resisteth the proud, but giveth grace unto the humble."*

Chapter Eleven

GOD'S KIND OF LOVE

Jesus said, *"Greater love hath no man than this, that a man lay down his life for his friends"* (John 15:13). God's definition of love is different from the world's definition. The world says love is finding someone who fulfills your needs and desires, but the focus of that kind of love is self. God's kind of love is not selfish. It lays down its life for another.

First Corinthians 13:3 says:

> *And though I bestow all my goods to feed the poor, and though I give my body to be burned, and have not charity, it profiteth me nothing.*

In other words, the motivation behind an act of "love" is more important than the action itself. You could give your life savings to feed the poor, but if you're doing it for self-gratification, it means nothing. You could even sacrifice your own life like jihadists and suicide bombers do, but if the motivation is to gain entrance into heaven with seventy virgins, that's not God's kind of love. If your motivation is not love, it profits nothing.

When God gives, He gives motivated by love. When God corrects, that too is motivated by His love for us. God does nothing out of selfish ambition or vain conceit (Phil. 2:3). First Corinthians describes His love like this:

> *Charity* [the unmerited, action-expressed love of God] *suffereth long, and is kind; charity envieth not; charity vaunteth not itself, is not puffed up, doth not behave itself unseemly, seeketh not her own, is not easily provoked, thinketh no evil; rejoiceth not in iniquity, but rejoiceth in the truth; beareth all things, believeth all things, hopeth all things, endureth all things. Charity never faileth.*
>
> **1 Corinthians 13:4–8**

God's love is humble. It is not puffed up. What most people today call love doesn't display any of the traits listed in 1 Corinthians. Their love is selfish and rude. It is easily angered and keeps record of wrongs. It envies and boasts and is quick to believe the worst in others. It doesn't resemble God's kind of love at all. At its best, it is a cheap imitation.

This is the reason so many marriages fail. You can't marry a person hoping they'll complete you or make your life perfect. Marriage is not about getting. It's not even a fifty-fifty endeavor. Marriage is about giving. If you want a lasting, happy marriage, find someone you can pour your life into and someone who will pour into you. See who can out-give and out-love the other.

If you love like God and put other people ahead of yourself, you'll not be easily provoked (1 Cor. 13:5). Remember Proverbs 13:10? It says, *"Only by pride cometh contention."* The only reason you get angry or give in to a "short fuse" is pride. I know that's hard to swallow, but it's the truth. You can't control what other people do. You may be praying for God to remove every obstacle, every person who rubs you the wrong way, but you're wasting your breath. Other people are not your problem. The way you respond to others and the circumstances of life is the problem. God called us to be salt and light in this world (Matt. 5:13–14). To do that, we have to get out of the saltshaker. We have to connect with others and love like God loves—humbly and selflessly.

> **What most people today call love doesn't display any of the traits listed in 1 Corinthians."**

Romans 1:18–20 says that God has given every man and woman an intuitive knowledge of their Creator. He draws each one with His love. But since the beginning, Satan has tried to divert man's attention from God. He has inspired some to deny

God's existence and harden their hearts to Him until they can no longer recognize His goodness or His rebuke (Rom. 1:28). Those who do acknowledge God, he tries to pervert and turn toward idolatry.

When Satan tempted Adam and Eve to disobey God in the Garden of Eden, he didn't threaten them. He didn't even start out lying. He was much subtler. Genesis says this:

> *Now the serpent was more subtil than any beast of the field which the LORD God had made. And he said unto the woman, Yea, hath God said, Ye shall not eat of every tree of the garden? And the woman said unto the serpent, We may eat of the fruit of the trees of the garden: but of the fruit of the tree which is in the midst of the garden, God hath said, Ye shall not eat of it, neither shall ye touch it, lest ye die. And the serpent said unto the woman, Ye shall not surely die: for God doth know that in the day ye eat thereof, then your eyes shall be opened, and ye shall be as gods, knowing good and evil.*

Genesis 3:1–5

That last statement was a boldfaced lie. But notice Satan didn't start there. Eve knew the command of God. So, Satan first got her to question God's intentions. He got her to question God's love. "You'll not surely die," he said. "God is holding out on you. He's trying to keep you from knowing good and evil. It would be better for you to break away from God. Do this your own way. Be like God. Be independent." And Genesis says she looked at the tree and saw that it was *"pleasant to the eyes"* and desirable to make one wise, so she yielded to Satan's temptation and took the fruit (Gen. 3:6). In a sense, she made herself God. That's the ultimate manifestation of pride.

God gave Adam and Eve the choice to follow Him. As free moral agents, He gives each of us the same choice. He will never force His will or ways upon us. That's part of His love. God allows us to choose. We can choose to respond to His love in humility and submit ourselves to Him, or we can choose to remain independent. But our independence is not without consequences. If we choose to remain independent of God, we're choosing to live independent of His protection, independent of His blessings, and independent of His grace.

Many people consider themselves "enlightened," viewing God's Word and the standards it contains as outdated. A few years ago, a US president, who claimed to be a Christian, endorsed several "lifestyle" choices that opposed God's Word. At a news conference, someone asked, "How can you claim to be a Christian and embrace modern values that contradict the Word of God?" He said, "The Bible is outdated. It may have originated from God, but it came through people. It was influenced by their society and tainted by their value system. It's no longer the pure Word of God."

He basically threw out the Word and exalted his own standards of righteousness. That's pride. But the day will come when every prideful person who has promoted values in opposition to the Word of God will see their error. I don't care if they were lauded by society or looked like they won in this life, a day will come when they will stand before God and answer for their pride. They will see the awesome glory of God and know their own foolishness. Those who have spit on the Word and insulted the grace of God will bow their knee in humiliation, admitting their wrong and confessing His Lordship (Phil. 2:10–11).

That day will come for all of us. But if we choose to respond to the love of God in this life, we won't be humiliated on that day. Instead, God will pour out His grace, saying, "Well done, good and faithful servant! Enter into the joy of the Lord" (see Matt. 25:21). We won't receive His grace because we did everything perfectly. God does not give grace based on a person's holiness; He gives it in proportion to their humility. If we choose to humble ourselves and put faith in Jesus, we will receive grace.

Humility loves what God loves and hates what God hates (Prov. 6:16–19). Notice that one of the things God hates is pride (Prov. 6:17). Humility submits to His standards and depends on Him. God's standard is love.

Jesus said unto him, Thou shalt love the Lord thy God with all thy heart, and with all thy soul, and with all thy mind. This is the first and great commandment. And the second is like unto it, Thou shalt love thy neighbour as thyself. On these two commandments hang all the law and the prophets.

Matthew 22:37–40

Loving God and loving others fulfills the law. But loving "thy neighour as thyself" does not mean ignoring their sin. Leviticus 19:17–18 says, *"Thou shalt not hate thy brother in thine heart: thou shalt in any wise rebuke thy neighbour, and not suffer sin upon him . . . Love thy neighbour as thyself: I am the* LORD.*"* To know God's standard, to know the truth, and not warn your neighbor of sin's consequences is wrong. It's not love.

> **Loving God and loving others fulfills the law. But loving 'thy neighour as thyself' does not mean ignoring their sin."**

Now, there are certainly wrong ways to correct your neighbor. We all know religious people who have used God's Word like a club to beat others. That's not what I'm talking about. Loving like God means hating what evil does to people—so much so that you set aside your own comfort to warn them.

I remember driving home one foggy night on a winding mountain road. It was dark. There were no streetlights. I could only see a short distance in front of me. A car passed me, slammed on its brakes, and jerked to the right. I could tell it hit something. I pulled to the side of the road and stopped. A few feet ahead lay an injured horse. Between the horse and our cars, all three lanes were blocked. But before I knew what was happening, another car came zooming around the bend and hit the horse. I could hear other cars coming up the road. With the fog, there was no way the drivers would see the wreck before it was too late, so I ran down the road to warn the people of the upcoming danger.

I jumped out at every car coming up the pass, waving my arms and shouting. I was honked at, yelled at, and cussed out. I'm sure everyone thought the worst of me, and honestly, it would have been easier to stay in my car and wait for the police. But if I hadn't tried to warn those people, I would have loved myself more than I loved my neighbor. I would have been more concerned with my own comfort than with their lives. Brothers and sisters, love speaks the truth, and love protects (1 Cor. 13:6–7, NIV).

Chapter Twelve

HUMILITY IS DEPENDENCE

True humility is simply dependence upon God. A friend of mine, Happy Caldwell, demonstrated this to me when he turned his church over to new pastors in 2014. He and his wife, Jeanne, planted Agape Church in Little Rock, Arkansas, in 1979. For thirty-five years, they poured their lives into that church, developing its ministries and investing their time and money. Agape was their whole life, but when God told them it was time to move on, they did. I heard Happy tell his story at a ministers' conference a few years back. He was encouraging older ministers to start thinking about transitioning their ministries to the next generation. During his invitation, he said, "Would you give up everything you've built if the Lord told you to go? Would you turn it over to someone else? Would you start over, or are you addicted to your security? Are you out to establish God's kingdom, or are you trying to establish your own?"

> **God is all I need. If I lost everything, if I was no longer on television, if we didn't have a Bible college, if I was back to square one, I would be okay."**

He was basically asking, "Are you humble?" As I stood there searching my heart, I prayed, "God, is there anything else You want me to do? Is there anything I need to set down? Is there anything I need to pick up?" I don't feel like the Lord told me to do anything different, but in that moment, I can truthfully say that I gave it all up. If God told me to go to Africa and start ministering from a grass hut, I'd do it. I'm not sure I could convince Jamie to go, but if God told me, I would willingly walk away from everything.

Psalm 27:4 says, *"One thing have I desired of the LORD, that will I seek after; that I may dwell in the house of the LORD all the days of my life, to behold the beauty of the LORD, and to enquire in his temple."* God is all I need. If I lost everything, if I was no longer on television, if we didn't have a Bible college, if I was back to square one, I would be okay.

To be humble, we must be willing to walk away from everything and everyone if that is what will please and glorify God. True humility doesn't have its own agenda. It's totally dependent on God. When Moses asked to see God's glory, the Lord replied, *"My presence shall go with thee, and I will give thee rest"* (Ex. 33:14). In the next verse, Moses expressed his complete dependence on God, basically saying, "Lord, if You don't go with me, I'm not moving!" That's humility. Humility seeks God. It recognizes that it can't do anything without Him.

Pride, on the other hand, refuses to recognize its dependence on God.

The wicked, through the pride of his countenance, will not seek after God: God is not in all his thoughts.

Psalm 10:4

Most people miss this part of humility. They think, *I'm not arrogant. I don't think I'm better than anyone else, so I must be humble.* But they don't depend on God. They don't seek Him unless they're in trouble. Most people only pray after exhausting every natural avenue. And while exhausting all natural resources before turning to God may be normal—meaning most people operate that way—it's not biblical. Most people believe you should do whatever you can do and then depend on God to do what you cannot. When someone gets sick, he or she explores all medical options before turning to God. I'm not saying Christians shouldn't use doctors or that doctors are evil. But as believers, shouldn't we believe God?

When it comes to finances, the Scriptures tell us to owe no one anything (Rom. 13:8). Yet how many Christians follow this instruction? Instead of depending on God as their source, they secure a loan and burn through thousands of dollars in interest. Then when they can't make their payments, they ask God to intervene. God is not a safety net or a fire extinguisher. He is God. Humility recognizes that and trusts Him to be who He said He is.

Jesus said, *"Verily, verily, I say unto you, The Son can do nothing of himself, but what he seeth the Father do: for what things soever he doeth, these also doeth the Son likewise"* (John 5:19). Some people have tried to use this statement to disprove Jesus's divinity, but I think it is one of the greatest proofs.

A few verses later, Jesus continued expressing His dependence on God, saying:

> *I can of mine own self do nothing: as I hear, I judge: and my judgment is just; because I seek not mine own will, but the will of the Father which hath sent me.*
>
> **John 5:30**

These types of statements demonstrate Jesus's oneness with the Father. Jesus so depended on God that He could not operate independently of Him. If Jesus Christ, the sinless Son of God, refused to operate outside humility, who do we think we are to try to do things on our own?

You may be a born-again Christian and love God, but are you living independently of Him? Are you doing things your own way and only turning to God when you fail? Or are you following the standards of His Word?

❝Jesus so depended on God that He could not operate independently of Him.❞

I've used this example before, but if God told you to attend Charis Bible College, why ask my opinion? Why seek my wisdom? If God tells you to do something, do it. I don't care if it harelips the devil or your mother, do it! It may not look like things will work out in your favor, but don't lean on your own understanding and fall into pride (Prov. 3:5). Trust God to be God and to work things out for your good (Is. 46:10 and Rom. 8:28).

When Peter saw Jesus walking on the water and said "Lord, if it's You, bid me come," and Jesus said to come; it was humility for Peter to obey (Matt. 14:28–29). It was humility for Peter to get out of the boat and walk on the water. Most people wouldn't see that as humility. They'd think a humble person would have kept quiet and stayed in the boat. But true humility believes God. It is dependent on Him and trusts His Word. If God tells you to stay in the boat, stay in the boat. But if God says "Come," doubting that Word (or your ability to perform it) would be pride. Peter's ability didn't allow him to walk on water. He walked on water because He trusted God's ability to perform His Word (Jer. 1:12).

Because God told me to build a Bible college, it is humility to obey. It is humility to trust God's ability to perform His Word to me, even though the price tag is upwards of $180 million. My natural tendency would be to say, "Oh God, who am I? How can I do this?" But that would be pride. That wouldn't be in agreement with His Word, which says, *"I can do all things through Christ which strengtheneth me"* (Phil. 4:13). For me, humility is saying what God said and doing what He told me to do. Some people misunderstand this. They criticize me and accuse me of building my own kingdom. Even some of my long-term partners have misunderstood my motives and stopped supporting me. But if I exalted my own opinion of how God could use me or was worried about the opinions and approval of people, I would be operating in pride.

I was raised with a wrong perception of humility. In my religious background, it was wrong to draw attention to myself. It was wrong to think highly of myself. If something good happened in my life, I was expected to deny it, saying, "I'm just an unworthy servant." That's the way I was raised. But the truth is, it is humility to acknowledge what God is doing at AWM and Charis.

If you grew up—like I did—with the impression that humility is a condemned, beat-down attitude of low self-esteem and therefore rejected some of the things God has told you to do, take a moment to repent. Humble yourself and allow the grace of God to flow in your life. If you've been timid, not stepping out and speaking your vision for fear of someone misunderstanding, repent. The only person you're out to please is God. God has asked you to do

> **❞ For me, humility is saying what God said and doing what He told me to do."**

something significant, something beyond your natural ability. I believe God has something for you to accomplish that will bless your family, your workplace, and your community. Don't allow pride to rob those people of His intended blessing. If God's place for you is collecting trash, fine. But if God wants you to be the owner of the trash company, accept that position. That's humility.

Humility is never something you get once and then walk in the rest of your life. It's a constant process of reevaluation and adjustment. I once heard a man say that he had dealt with his flesh twenty years earlier and had no problem with pride. The moment he said that, I called him "Ichabod" in my mind. The name Ichabod basically means the glory has departed. That man was in pride and didn't even realize it! Paul said:

And if any man think that he knoweth any thing, he knoweth nothing yet as he ought to know.

1 Corinthians 8:2

No one can cast out pride. The only way to get rid of it completely is to die. As long as we live in a body, we have to deal with self. We have to manage the tendency within ourselves to operate independently of God.

My dad used to say, "He who tooteth not his own horn, the same shall not be tooted." But that idea is not a godly concept. It ignores what God's Word says about promotion (Ps. 75:6–7) and disregards God's instruction to humble ourselves (James 4:10). It doesn't trust His promise to reward those who serve *"as to the Lord"* or who seek first His kingdom (Eph. 6:7–8, Col. 3:23–24, and Matt. 6:33). That line of thinking exposes a belief that God is indifferent, that we cannot depend on His help, that He won't reward us for walking in humility. But nothing could be further from the truth!

Chapter Thirteen

A FAITHFUL WITNESS

Many people don't trust God to care for their needs or perform His Word. So, they spend all their energy promoting themselves and seeing to their own needs. True humility is in terribly short supply, even among those who should know better. I run into ministers all the time who can't carry on a conversation except to brag about their accomplishments. In order to secure man's acceptance, they take credit for what God is doing. But that is wrong.

A truly humble person gives God glory. God is the source of everything good in our lives (James 1:17). You may have worked hard for your money, but God gave you the power to get wealth (Deut. 8:18). You may have put in hours at the gym, but God knit you together in your mother's womb (Ps. 139:13). You may have developed your skills in music and art until your fingers were calloused and bleeding, but God gave you that talent to bless and serve others (1 Pet. 4:10). No one is a self-made man or woman.

Many years ago, before I was on television, I had radio broadcasts throughout Texas. From one of those broadcasts, I received an invitation to be interviewed during a well-known minister's television show. This minister had a large church in the Dallas-Fort Worth area, so while I was in town, I attended his Sunday morning service. Now, I'd been ministering on radio for about a decade, but no one knew my face, and I started wondering how many of the four or five thousand people in his church had heard my broadcast. I wondered if they would recognize my voice or know who I was. I began imagining all the ones I'd ministered to, and I started to take credit for their maturity. (Now, I'm not proud of this story, but I think it illustrates a powerful point.) As I was sitting there thinking these things, the Lord spoke to my heart. "Andrew," He said, "that's pride. You didn't touch these people's lives; I did. The words I've given you are not for your glory. They're for Mine."

> **You didn't touch these people's lives; I did. The words I've given you are not for your glory. They're for Mine."**

While the Lord was rebuking me, the pastor of that church asked me to stand. "We're so glad to have Andrew Wommack in the congregation today," he said. And in that moment, I felt like God was shining a spotlight on my pride. I felt exposed, naked. Of course, the Lord didn't expose me to any of those people; no one knew what I'd been thinking. But boy, was it uncomfortable! When we take the credit for what God has done, we steal His glory and set ourselves up for humiliation.

> *I am the LORD: that is my name: and my glory will I not give to another, neither my praise to graven images.*
>
> **Isaiah 42:8**

Now, there is balance to this. You can steal God's glory by taking credit for what He's done, but you can also steal His glory by not giving Him credit or allowing others to honor what He's done in you. God has used me. He has touched many lives through me. It's not pride to acknowledge that, as long as I am giving the glory to God. He is the source.

Jesus never took glory for Himself. In John 5:30, when He said, *"I can of mine own self do nothing: as I hear, I judge: and my judgment is just; because I seek not mine own will, but the will of the Father which hath sent me,"* Jesus was expressing His dependence on God, but He was also glorifying His Father. "My Father is the one speaking," He said. "I only say what He says."

Once when Jesus was teaching in the temple, the people asked, "Where does this man get all His wisdom? Isn't He Joseph's son? He never went to seminary . . ." Here's how Jesus responded:

> *My doctrine is not mine, but his that sent me. If any man will do his will, he shall know of the doctrine, whether it be of God, or whether I speak of myself. He that speaketh of himself seeketh his own glory: but he that seeketh his glory that sent him, the same is true, and no unrighteousness is in him.*
>
> **John 7:16–18**

Jesus didn't speak His own message. He was a faithful witness and credited God for His wisdom.

A man I respect recently came to me about some doctrinal issues he had been researching. He was convinced God had shown him some things, but he was struggling to prove them scripturally. What he said made sense, but in order to come to his conclusions, he had to go outside the Bible. Now, I'm not saying that everything outside the Bible is wrong, but I just can't trust things outside the Bible like I trust the Bible. So, I told him, "Everything you said makes sense. It may be absolutely true, but if it can't be verified by Scripture, I will never teach it."

We can't start basing our doctrine on things outside the Word of God. It would be like building a house without a foundation. It may look pretty for a while, but eventually that house will crumble. There's nothing there to sustain it. Some people have said, "This is deep. It goes beyond the Word." Man, if you're beyond the Word, you're too deep for me! I'm going to stick with the Word. I'm not going to invent my own doctrines or seek my own glory. I'm going to build on the foundation of the Word.

There was no unrighteousness in Jesus. He was humble. He didn't seek His own glory, but He

> **There's nothing wrong with acknowledging the good things God has given you or done in you. The question is, are you giving God the glory?"**

didn't deny the good things He did; He simply gave His Father the credit. There's a false impression about humility that people should downplay and discredit their accomplishments. But that's not really humility. That's a religious con. There's nothing wrong with acknowledging the good things God has given you or done in you. The question is, are you giving God the glory? Do you recognize Him as the source?

Taking credit for all the good in your life, saying, "Look at me; look what I've done," is pride. But downplaying what God has done through you is also pride. You're essentially stealing His glory. Jesus didn't downplay the miracles God did through Him. He didn't deny that the dead were raised, the blind received their sight, or the lame walked. He even cited those miracles as proof of who He was (Matt. 11:4–6). But every time someone asked, "Where did You get this authority?" He gave glory to God. He was a faithful witness (Rev. 1:5).

The book of Proverbs says a lot about a faithful witness or a faithful and trustworthy messenger (Prov. 13:17; 14:5, 25; and 25:13). A faithful witness is true to the one who sent them. They're not out to glorify themselves but to represent, with accuracy and dependability, the one who sent them. An unfaithful messenger is more concerned with his or her own reputation. If the message they are to deliver could cause them personal injury or embarrassment, an unfaithful messenger will modify the message to ensure it is (and they are) well received. That's pride.

A Barna survey said that ninety percent of all ministers believe the Word of God addresses every social ill and moral problem in our society, but that same survey reveals less than ten percent of ministers will preach the answers from the pulpit. They know what the Word says, but they won't teach it for fear that attendance or offerings will decline. They won't teach the truth because they might get hate mail or have blogs written about them. They only preach uncontroversial things or things that will advance their position. That's being an unfaithful witness. That's seeking the praise and acceptance of man rather than God. This isn't only a problem for ministers; pew-sitters do it too. Though they know what the Word of God says, they stay quiet so they won't be criticized and rejected. That's why our nation is in turmoil—Christians are silent. They're not being salt and light (Matt. 5:13–14). They're not being faithful witnesses.

I remember ministering in Germany once through an interpreter. I didn't know the language or culture, so I had to trust this interpreter to convey my message in a way the people would understand. I'm not sure exactly how to describe what I felt, but I could tell I wasn't connecting. Even though it seemed like I had the people's attention, they weren't responding. And that is very unusual in my meetings! Typically when I speak, people either love it or hate it. I never get a lukewarm reception. This meeting was frustrating to me. I just couldn't figure out what was wrong. So, after the first session, I spoke to the pastor. "What's going on?" I said. "Things just aren't working."

"The interpreter is not doing his job," he said. "He's changing what you're saying because he doesn't agree with you. He doesn't believe the Bible really says what you say it says."

You could phrase that a lot of ways, but it is pride. The interpreter was worried people wouldn't like what he had to say. He was more concerned with his reputation than mine and misrepresented what I said. He shouldn't have even considered what the people thought of him; he wasn't interpreting for himself. He was interpreting for me. If the people didn't like what I was saying through him, the criticism wouldn't have gone to him. It would've gone to me. In a sense, that's what ministers do when they don't represent (literally re-present) the whole counsel of God's Word. They misinterpret for the Lord. As a faithful witness, they shouldn't concern themselves with how people respond. They shouldn't be seeking their own glory or worrying about their reputation. A faithful witness will just say what God says and let the chips fall where they may.

Years ago, I ministered on finances at a meeting where the people there were so receptive it was like pouring water on parched ground. The next Sunday, one of the pastors who invited me to the meeting repented in front of his entire congregation. He got down on his knees and apologized to the people, saying, "I'm so sorry. I knew the things Andrew taught on finances and have personally operated in them for years, but I've never spoken them from this pulpit for fear of offending you. I didn't want you to think ill of me or believe I was only after your money. I was wrong for not teaching you this part of God's Word. Please forgive me." And as he humbled himself, the people in his church ran forward, throwing money on the stage. In one service, they paid off all the church's indebtedness!

In a moment of humility, that pastor became a faithful witness. He wasn't worried about promoting himself or protecting his reputation. He wasn't trying to build his own kingdom. He became a faithful witness, and according to Proverbs 25:13, he *"refresh*[ed] *the soul"* of God.

Chapter Fourteen

THE KEY TO PROMOTION

Andrew Wommack Ministries and Charis Bible College employs well over 650 people worldwide. At every level within the organization, we look to hire and promote faithful witnesses. An unfaithful witness would misuse the power and authority given them and would hurt the ministry, so we're constantly evaluating a person's trustworthiness. When a person messes up—and everyone does—do they acknowledge the truth and deal with it, or do they make excuses to cover it up? Do they exaggerate or manipulate the facts (Prov. 14:5)? If so, then that person is more concerned with their own reputation than with the ministry's. Their heart isn't interested in serving; they're only at AWM to launch their own ministry or for some other reason. We still love them, but it lowers their value to us because we cannot entrust them with more authority. They aren't a faithful witness.

But when a person does what is right for the ministry, even if it works out to their detriment, that speaks volumes about their character. That man (or woman) becomes one of our most valuable assets.

> *Likewise, ye younger, submit yourselves unto the elder. Yea, all of you be subject one to another, and be clothed with humility: for God resisteth the proud, and giveth grace to the humble.*
>
> **1 Peter 5:5**

God loves us regardless of whether we're doing things right, but God cannot promote pride. And the more like God I get, the more grace I give to people who humble themselves. Those who are self-serving and insecure, who manipulate circumstances and blame others to exalt self, those people I resist. That doesn't mean I treat them badly. But like God, I can't promote that. I need faithful witnesses.

Years ago, I had an employee named Milton Ooley. He ran my IT department. As the ministry began to grow, Milton needed help. We posted the job opportunity and got an application from a man in Phoenix, Arizona. I had a meeting down there, so Milton and I traveled to Phoenix together. The plan was for Milton to interview the applicant, Stan Priest, while I was at the meeting and then find a computer to check his proficiency levels. When I got back after the service, I asked Milton about it.

"The man is a genius," he said. "I never did give him a test. After talking with him for a few minutes, I figured he had forgotten more about computers than I would ever know!"

Needless to say, we hired Stan. He started working for us in the data entry department. I didn't know it at the time, but that was a huge step down for him. He had been running the entire IT department at Food for the Hungry. After we hired Stan, his old boss came to town and took me out to eat. "I came to try to hire Stan back," he said. "We need him. We had to hire a recruiter to find someone to fill his position. And even then, we only found two people in the whole country who are qualified to do what he was doing."

Stan has been a tremendous blessing to the ministry. He and his wife, Donna, have been with us for over thirty years now. Shortly after we hired Stan, Milton quit his job and moved back to Texas. "Stan is so much better at this than I am," he said. "He can take you places I can't."

Milton was not out to promote himself. He wasn't seeking his own glory. He wanted what was best for the ministry, and when someone else came along more qualified than he was, Milton willingly stepped aside. That is a godly attitude. Yet many people would not have the character to do something like that. If they saw someone more qualified in an organization, they would feel threatened. They would do anything to hide that person's talents or push them out of the way. They would misrepresent things to make the other person look bad. They might even steal their ideas. You can call that a lot of different things. Some might even call it job security. But it's really just pride. A person like that is out to glorify self.

Jesus could say His judgment was just because He didn't seek His own glory (John 5:30). He lived to bring glory to God. This is the attitude God promotes.

Gary Luecke ran Charis Colorado for years before being promoted to manage Charis worldwide. He later stepped down to follow the Lord's leading, but for years he told us, "Whatever you want me to do, however the ministry can use me, I'm willing." When he first came to work for us, he took a huge cut in pay. But he wasn't in it for the money. He came because he felt like that was what God called him to do.

Greg Mohr is now our Charis director. I've known Greg and Janice for decades. I used to minister in their church. But when Greg came to Charis, he didn't ask for a specific position. Even though he had pastored for twenty-seven years, he didn't ask for authority. He just said, "I am here to serve and be a blessing to this ministry. I'll do whatever you need me to do." So, we used him to fill an open position.

A few years later, Greg approached me and said, "I believe God is leading me into more of a leadership role at Charis. But I'm here to serve. If you want me to stay in my current position, I'll do it, and I'll do it with a good attitude. But I feel this is what God has gifted me in." That was humility. Greg wasn't out to promote himself. He was willing to serve wherever, but when he felt God nudging his heart, he responded.

(He told me later that while he was a student at Rhema, God had spoken to him and told him that one day he would run a Bible college. At the time, he thought maybe God meant Rhema. But decades later, he realized God was talking about Charis.) Now, Greg didn't come to me playing the God card. He wasn't trying to manipulate me into promoting him by saying "God said." He spent several years just serving, letting us see his heart and character. He really worked his way into a position of leadership.

Barry Bennett, who is now our Dean of Instructors at CBC, has been a successful missionary in Chile and headed a Spanish-speaking Bible school in Texas. He is a very qualified minister and one of the most favorite teachers we have. But he didn't come to work for me tooting his own horn and telling us we need to use him in the college. He worked in our communication services department for two years answering my emails.

In conversation some of my employees found out his background and asked him to take a chapel service in CBC. The students loved it. They gave him a standing ovation and then bought more of his CDs than anyone we had speak up to that point.

Once during a transition period, I asked Barry if he was interested in taking the directorship of Charis. He said he didn't feel that was his gifting. He turned down an increase in salary and authority because he wanted only what the Lord had for him. That's a faithful man.

I could go down the list of our Charis leadership team and talk about this attitude in each one on the team. Paul Milligan, the man who used to run our ministry, recently told me, "If you're ever finished with me, if you ever feel like someone else could do these things, I'm free to go. You'll not hurt my feelings. I'm just here to serve." That's humility. All these people are serving a greater purpose than themselves. They're not out to build their own kingdom. They are just doing what they believe is right. They are serving God and are faithful to whomever God puts in authority over them. And that's what makes a faithful witness.

If we would get this attitude, serving heartily as unto the Lord—even for the ungodly—God would reward us (Eph. 6:8). The psalmist said:

> *For promotion cometh neither from the east, nor from the west, nor from the south. But God is the judge: he putteth down one, and setteth up another.*
>
> **Psalm 75:6–7**

Promotion comes from God. Whether or not a boss sees and promotes humility, God does. He causes the humble to receive favor with their current boss, find a better job, or build their own business. For some people, the very reason they haven't been promoted is this issue of humility. They've not been a faithful witness. They're only out to glorify and promote themselves. They manipulate facts. They're envious of their coworkers and can't speak peaceably about anyone. They won't do what is right if it means they could lose.

I remember a fundraising company coming to me years ago and promising a return of $1 million if I would let them write a fundraising letter for me. The ministry was only making probably $200,000 a year at that point, so I asked, "How are you going to do that?" They explained their process to me (and they had it down to a science), but everything they wanted to write in the letter was dishonest and manipulative.

"None of that is true," I said.

"It doesn't matter if it's true," they told me. "You're doing great things here. Let us get you the money so you can do even more. The end justifies the means."

"No, it doesn't!" I said as I kicked them out. "I don't need money that badly."

Brothers and sisters, the end does not justify the means! We need to do what is right. We need to do things with humility, which is submission to and dependence on Him.

I once knew a man, a very godly man who loved the Lord, who struggled with lying. When he was very young, his father beat him over the smallest infraction, so he learned to lie to save his hide—literally. He would do whatever it took to please his

> **We need to do what is right. We need to do things with humility, which is submission to and dependence on Him."**

father and avoid a beating. And without realizing it, he carried that childhood survival tactic into adulthood. As a grown man, he would say the stupidest things. He would lie at the drop of a hat. He would exaggerate and misrepresent things just to impress people. No one could trust what he said, and it eventually cost him his job.

People call that a spirit of lying, but it's really a spirit of pride. It's being insecure and afraid of people's rejection. It's trying to avoid pain. A person like that is afraid the truth won't benefit them, so they only present a portion of it. When they do that, they're bearing false witness (Ex. 20:16), and that's pride. They're not working *as to the Lord* (Eph. 6:7). They're working for self. And they wonder why things aren't working out. Grace—favor and promotion—can only flow through humility (James 4:6).

Chapter Fifteen

JESUS—OUR EXAMPLE

Jesus is our greatest example of humility. He didn't worry about what was popular or stress about man's approval. He just did what God told Him to do and gave credit to His Father. After Jesus fed the 5,000 with five loaves and two fish, the people were so amazed, they wanted to make Him king (John 6). But Jesus *"knew what was in man"* (John 2:25). He knew the people's hearts weren't with Him. They weren't worshiping and following Him because He was God; they followed Him because He filled their bellies. It was all selfish. They thought Jesus was the ticket to meeting their needs. So, Jesus began preaching a hard message.

> *Labour not for the meat which perisheth, but for that meat which endureth unto everlasting life, which the Son of man shall give unto you: for him hath God the Father sealed. Then said they unto him, What shall we do, that we might work the*

works of God? Jesus answered and said unto them, This is the work of God, that ye believe on him whom he hath sent.

John 6:27–29

After Jesus spoke these words, the people demanded a sign from Him. They wanted Him to produce manna and feed them, like Moses fed the Israelites in the wilderness (John 6:30-31). Jesus had miraculously fed 5,000 men—not including women and children—the day before, but that wasn't enough for them. So, He replied:

Verily, verily, I say unto you, Moses gave you not that bread from heaven; but my Father giveth you the true bread from heaven. For the bread of God is he which cometh down from heaven, and giveth life unto the world.

John 6:32–33

Jesus said, "You're looking for manna from heaven, but I am the Bread of Life. God sent me to give life to the world." I'm sure people in Jesus's day thought that statement was arrogant. But it was the truth. It was humility for Jesus to declare Himself to be the Bread of Life. He was agreeing with His Father.

It's not wrong to speak the truth. If you've built a billion-dollar company, it's not humility to deny what you've done. That's a religious con. True humility would say, "Yes, I built a billion-dollar company, but God gave me the opportunity. He gave me the wisdom to build well. I'm glad this company can be a blessing and employ so many people." Humility doesn't deny good things. It just gives God credit.

I've seen multiple people raised from the dead throughout the history of my ministry. Yet people criticize me and accuse me of promoting myself when I tell those stories. I never claim to perform those miracles; I can't raise a gnat! God raised my son from the dead. God raised my wife. God raised up the man from Pritchett. That's not pride. That's what God said would happen (Mark 16:17–18 and John 14:12). That is glorifying God.

> **❝ And it's humility to acknowledge them—as long as I give God glory and don't take credit for myself."**

Humility does not debase or criticize self, nor does it refuse to acknowledge the good in your life. God has done some amazing things in my life. And it's humility to acknowledge them—as long as I give God glory and don't take credit for myself. That's what Jesus was doing when He said:

> *I am the bread of life: he that cometh to me shall never hunger; and he that believeth on me shall never thirst. But I said unto you, That ye also have seen me, and believe not. All that the Father giveth*

*me shall come to me; and him that cometh to me
I will in no wise cast out. For I came down from
heaven, not to do mine own will, but the will of
him that sent me.*

John 6:35–38

Jesus didn't come to the earth to seek His own will. He was busy building His Father's kingdom. He said, *"This is the will of him that sent me, that every one which seeth the Son, and believeth on him, may have everlasting life: and I will raise him up at the last day"* (John 6:40). But the Jews murmured at Jesus's words (John 6:41). They questioned His motives, and some even labeled Him a heretic. They said, *"Is not this Jesus, the son of Joseph, whose father and mother we know? how is it then that he saith, I came down from heaven?"* (John 6:42).

What Jesus said was true. He did come down from heaven. He wasn't an ordinary man. He was God manifesting in the flesh (John 1:1; 1 Tim. 3:16), and it would have been pride for Jesus to deny that. It would have been pride to temper His words for fear of the people's response.

That's the problem with modern-day ministers. The vast majority of them do not speak the truth about finances, healing, and the baptism of the Holy Spirit for fear someone will misunderstand or criticize. Others refuse to address what God says about marriage, parenting, and sexual purity for the same reason. They think God's Word is too strong for society to handle, so they water it down to make it more palatable. They quit being a faithful witness, and they start interjecting their own words and ideas.

People who are afraid of criticism, who need the approval and validation of people, are proud. Proverbs 29:25 says, *"The fear of man bringeth a snare."* A snare is a trap used to catch an animal. Satan uses the fear of man to snare or trap us in pride. This fear is rooted in selfishness. If you are going to represent God, you must be prepared for criticism (2 Tim. 3:12). Jesus said, *"Woe to you when everyone speaks well of you, for that is how their ancestors treated the false prophets"* (Luke 6:26, NIV). If you aren't being persecuted, you aren't living godly or truly representing God. If you never bump into the devil, it's because you're both headed in the same direction.

> ❝ If you aren't being persecuted, you aren't living godly or truly representing God. If you never bump into the devil, it's because you're both headed in the same direction."

When you start representing God, it will cost you something. Jesus asked, *"If they have called the master of the house Beelzebub, how much more shall they call them of his household?"* (Matt. 10:25). When you share the unadulterated Word of God and people misunderstand, don't fall all over yourself to apologize or explain what you said. When the people misunderstood Jesus and began murmuring, He didn't backpedal. He said:

Murmur not among yourselves. No man can come to me, except the Father which hath sent me draw him: and I will raise him up at the last day. It is written in the prophets, And they shall be all taught of God. Every man therefore that hath heard, and hath learned of the Father, cometh unto me. Not that any man hath seen the Father, save he which is of God, he hath seen the Father.

John 6:43b–46

Jesus basically said, "Why are you murmuring? None of your teachers have firsthand knowledge of what they speak about, but I do. I'm the only one who has seen the Father, and I can speak with authority about Him." Jesus continued:

Verily, verily, I say unto you, He that believeth on me hath everlasting life. I am that bread of life. Your fathers did eat manna in the wilderness, and are dead. This is the bread which cometh down from heaven, that a man may eat thereof, and not die. I am the living bread which came down from heaven: if any man eat of this bread, he shall live for ever: and the bread that I will give is my flesh, which I will give for the life of the world.

John 6:47–51

The Jews completely missed the spiritual application of Jesus's words. They thought He spoke of cannibalism (John 6:52). If this sort of misunderstanding were to happen today, most ministers would go out of their way to explain themselves and keep from offending anyone. But Jesus just made it worse, saying:

> *Verily, verily, I say unto you, Except ye eat the flesh of the Son of man, and drink his blood, ye have no life in you. Whoso eateth my flesh, and drinketh my blood, hath eternal life; and I will raise him up at the last day. For my flesh is meat indeed, and my blood is drink indeed. He that eateth my flesh, and drinketh my blood, dwelleth in me, and I in him.*

John 6:53–56

To put this into a modern-day context, let's say I was drawing crowds of 20,000 people at one of my Gospel Truth Conferences. Then God told me to preach something unpopular, something that would weed out the people and narrow the crowds to those who were really committed to Him. And let's say many people got offended at what I preached, and 18,000 left. Boy, would I be the talk of the town! People would say, "Did you hear about Andrew Wommack? He had 20,000 people coming to his meetings, and he blew it! People were getting up and walking out; he offended everyone. Only a handful are left." People would say I was a failure. I'm sure many looked at Jesus as a failure too.

Even Jesus's disciples began murmuring at His words. *"Doth this offend you?"* He asked (John 6:61). *"It is the spirit that quickeneth; the flesh profiteth nothing: the words that I speak unto you, they are spirit, and they are life. But there are some of you that believe not"* (John 6:63–64). Jesus knew what was in their hearts. He knew that many followed Him for what they could get out of Him. They followed Him for the food, the miracles, and the prestige. So, Jesus began to place an expectation on His followers. He basically said, "You have to follow Me for more than what I can do for you. If you really want to experience the kingdom of God, you have to truly believe."

What happened next?

> *From that time many of his disciples went back, and walked no more with him.*
>
> **John 6:66**

Spiritually speaking, followers of Jesus must partake of Him to live. There is no other way to the Father (Acts 4:12). The Jews didn't understand that, and Jesus didn't try to explain. He didn't put their concerns to rest or correct their assumptions. He wasn't concerned with what they thought of Him. He was out to glorify His Father, not Himself. Jesus was a faithful witness. He remained true to what the Father had to say whether or not it worked to His benefit.

Chapter Sixteen

TRUE SUCCESS

Not many Christians—or even ministers—are sold out to God's will. People say, "I'm ready to serve God, but I hope He doesn't send me to Africa to live in a grass hut!" In other words, they're willing to serve God to an extent. But humility does not have limits on obedience. True humility seeks to glorify God even when it looks like you might personally lose.

In my opinion, Jesus displayed a greater humility—a greater dependence on God—when the multitudes left than at any other point in His earthly ministry. Think about it. He was successful. The people loved Him. They wanted to make Him king. Many believed He was the Messiah (at least what they thought the Messiah would be). But when Jesus preached that hard message in John 6 and many left, He didn't waver. He didn't change His message or seek to renew their favor. He didn't perform another miracle.

Though most would look at Jesus in that moment and say He had failed, I believe it was one of His greatest hours—even greater than His triumphant entry into Jerusalem (John 12). He wasn't fazed by the rejection of others. His love for, and commitment to, the Father didn't change. He even turned to the Twelve and asked, "Are you going too?" Jesus wasn't codependent on people's approval. He just kept doing what His Father told him to do, regardless of the people's response.

I'm currently in a season of life and ministry where God is blessing my socks off. People are responding. Lives are being changed. It's awesome! But it wasn't too long ago that Jamie and I were struggling, that I served God without any visible proof that what I was doing was making a difference. So, I'm not codependent on what we're currently seeing in the ministry. If people were to stop responding, if we lost everything, I would be okay. I would still have my relationship with God.

I remember a time when my board counseled me to shut down the ministry. They were looking over our finances, comparing our donations to our debts, and basically told me I was bankrupt. "We have to shut the ministry down," they said. "As good stewards, we can't let this continue. You're in trouble. It's not working. You need to get out of the ministry."

To be honest, there was a part of me that rejoiced. I thought, *God, I can go back to pouring concrete for a living. I don't have to worry about paying the bills, expanding my partner base, or meeting my employees' needs. I can just focus on relationship with You. I can focus on relationship with Jamie and the kids. This will be awesome!* But I knew that wasn't God's will for me, and instead of voicing those thoughts, I said, "I know this is what God told me to do, so let's pray about it. He has the answer."

As we prayed, the phone rang. It was my mother. She was opening the ministry mail at the time,

> **❝I said, 'I know this is what God told me to do, so let's pray about it. He has the answer.'"**

and she called to tell me we had just received a $60,000 offering. Some church where I had never ministered sent enough money to cover every debt and meet the ministry's needs for the next month!

The point is, losing everything would not devastate me. I'm committed. I've faced this before, and I can truthfully say that I could walk away from it all. God is my source. Relationship with Him is what makes me tick, and I evaluate my success by that relationship.

But most people evaluate success on external, natural things. They don't equate humility and following God's will as success. They want to know how much money you have, how big your buildings are, and how many people you're reaching. Most people would do anything to meet those criteria and secure man's approval.

I know of a man who came up with a "new way" of doing church a few years back. He wanted to attract large crowds and avoid offending anyone. So, he made his sermons short and illustrated, made the music concert-like with smoke and lights, and hid prayer in a back room. He thought once he got people through the doors, he could disciple them in small groups throughout the week. He called his idea being "seeker friendly," but it was more performance than ministry. Don't get me wrong. People came. Books were written and interviews given. He was labeled a "success." Thousands of churches across the country bought into his program. But I heard that by his own admission, it didn't work. Ministry became a mile wide and an inch deep. They weren't making disciples.

Unfortunately, the majority of ministers fall into this trap. They want to be respected. They want to make a difference. So, they'll try anything to increase numbers and boost offerings. They begin promoting themselves, and when the numbers come, they do whatever it takes to maintain that advantage and protect their reputation. They stop accurately representing God. They stop speaking the truth.

If anyone had the right to promote themselves, it was Jesus. Yet Jesus was humble. In John 14:10, Jesus said, *"Believest thou not that I am in the Father, and the Father in me? the words that I speak unto you I speak not of myself: but the Father that dwelleth in me, he doeth the works."* Jesus never promoted Himself. He never operated independently of His Father but always spoke the words God gave Him. And when those words brought Him acclaim, He gave God credit.

Even when the people left Jesus, it didn't faze Him. He didn't suck His thumb or complain that everyone hated Him and had hurt His feelings. Jesus knew what was in their hearts. He knew their praise was fickle, but it didn't matter. He wasn't out to glorify Himself. He wanted to glorify His Father, and if He felt His Father's pleasure, it didn't matter who rejected Him. Jesus didn't gain His self-worth from the people's acceptance. He wasn't concerned by their desertion. He wanted a commitment level that was genuine—heartfelt. Most churches don't have those standards.

I once overheard a man trying to lead a woman through the prayer of salvation. When he got to the part of her confession that Jesus rose from the dead, she stopped and said, "I can't say that."

"Why not?" he asked.

"Because I don't believe Jesus rose from the dead. I don't believe He's alive."

And the man said, "Well, pray it anyway. It doesn't matter whether you believe."

I had to intervene. "It does matter," I said. "Romans says to confess with your mouth the Lord Jesus and believe in your heart that God raised Him from the dead. A person must do that before they can be saved" (Rom. 10:9).

Some churches I visit give mass invitations. They invite those who want to commit their lives to Christ to come to the altar. Then they add, "If you've not lived up to your commitment and have fallen away from the Lord, come down and rededicate your life." And they just keep going: "If you're struggling . . . if you chew gum . . . if you breathe . . . come on down." People who have served God for thirty years respond and are lumped into the numbers of new converts. That's not integrity; that's headhunting. That's like going out to witness and coming back with scalps on your belt and saying, "I led all these people to the Lord!" We need to represent God accurately and minister to people out of a pure heart, not try to build our own kingdom or improve our statistics.

Before the Lord touched my life, I used to do that. I went witnessing every Tuesday and Thursday, and each week I'd stand in front of the church to report on the number of people I'd led to the Lord. I didn't do what I did because I loved God or because I loved people. I was trying to gain God's acceptance. I was depending on the people's accolades to boost my self-worth. When I finally got turned on to the Lord, I quit keeping track. It was no longer about me. I wanted people to know about the God I loved. I wanted to see them experience His love and salvation for *their* benefit.

Isaiah 48:11 says, *"For mine own sake, even for mine own sake, will I do it: for how should my name be polluted? and I will not give my glory unto another."* As I've said before, God will not share His glory with another. He will not allow His name to be polluted. God loves us (Rom. 5:5). He has called each of us to *"the obtaining of the glory of our Lord Jesus Christ"* (2 Thess. 2:14). He has given us the Holy Spirit and empowered us with the same authority Jesus had as His Son. But He has not done these things to glorify us. He is bringing glory to His Son (John 17:1).

Long ago, the Lord told me He was not out to promote me. As long as I was pointing people to Jesus and making His name known—sharing the Word and speaking the truth that set people free—God would promote me and expand the ministry so we could reach new people. The goal was not to glorify me; it was to glorify Jesus.

Many wonder why God doesn't open doors of promotion for them, and this is often the reason. Their goal is not to promote Jesus; they only wish to glorify themselves. God knows this. He understands the temptation we face to seek credit, to promote ourselves and guarantee our best interests. Until we learn to disciple ourselves in humility, He won't put us into positions of leadership. It would destroy us. It would hurt those around us. We wouldn't be able to handle the temptation of pride—and God loves us too much to allow that.

> **Many wonder why God doesn't open doors of promotion for them, and this is often the reason. Their goal is not to promote Jesus; they only wish to glorify themselves."**

Chapter Seventeen

GOD'S CHOICE

To recap, humility is God-dependence. True humility doesn't lean on its own understanding (Prov 3:5) but believes and obeys the Word. It doesn't do its own thing and then pray to escape the consequences of bad decisions. Humility goes to God first. Psalm 10:4 says, *"The wicked, through the pride of his countenance, will not seek after God: God is not in all his thoughts."* A prideful person will not seek God. They won't concern themselves with God's ways or thoughts unless those ways can further their own desires.

Pride, or independence from God, was Satan's original sin. Satan refused to do things God's way, and He tried to hoard God's glory for himself. True humility gives God glory. It doesn't promote self. It doesn't crave attention or worry about others' opinions. It speaks the truth and is immune to man's rejection and criticism. Like Moses, humility says, "Lord, if You don't go with me, I'm not moving! I can't do anything without You" (Ex. 33:15).

> **" God chooses the humble. He chooses those who will depend on Him, who know they are nothing without Him."**

God chooses the humble. He chooses those who will depend on Him, who know they are nothing without Him. People who think, *I can handle it. God, if You would manage the introduction, I can take it from there,* are proud. The apostle Paul said:

For ye see your calling, brethren, how that not many wise men after the flesh, not many mighty, not many noble, are called: but God hath chosen the foolish things of the world to confound the wise; and God hath chosen the weak things of the world to confound the things which are mighty; and base things of the world, and things which are despised, hath God chosen, yea, and things which are not, to bring to nought things that are: that no flesh should glory in his presence.

1 Corinthians 1:26–29

We have to recognize that we can do nothing without God (John 15:5), but we need to balance that with the truth that we are never without God (Heb. 13:5). Religion has taught that we must deny every good thing we have or have accomplished, but that is false humility. True humility acknowledges the good and acknowledges where that good originated.

It is not humility to deny the truth. Jesus said, *"I know him* [speaking of His Father]: *and if I should say, I know him not, I shall be a liar like unto you"* (John 8:55). There's nothing wrong with acknowledging the good things God has given you. If someone's life has been changed through your ministry, if you've succeeded in business or raised a godly family, if you've blessed an employer with good work, there's nothing wrong with acknowledging that. Just be humble. Humility glorifies God in all things without denying the good He has done through you.

For example, if a person won a track meet, it would be wrong for that person to say, "Oh, I didn't do anything," when people congratulated them for their win. If they won the track meet, they won the track meet. There's nothing wrong with acknowledging that, as long as that person also acknowledges God, who gave them the talent and health to compete.

A person of humility is secure. It's hard to offend them. It's hard to threaten a person who's not trying to build their own kingdom. No matter what people say about them or threaten to take from them, they don't care. They know no one can take away their relationship with God or nullify His Word, and nothing else matters to them. God can use someone like that.

Joshua, Moses's aide, was given charge of leading the Israelite community after Moses's death. Moses was respected within the community. God had used him to bring the Israelites out of slavery in Egypt. Moses had led the people through the Red Sea. He'd guided them through the desert and brought water from a rock. He had spoken with God face to face, given the people the Law, and crushed internal rebellions. Moses was a hard act to follow! But Joshua had proven himself a faithful witness. For forty years, he'd served Moses. He'd accepted his position as God-given and hadn't tried to usurp authority. He was humble, and in Joshua 1, the Lord told him:

> *Moses my servant is dead; now therefore arise, go over this Jordan, thou, and all this people, unto the land which I do give to them, even to the children of Israel. Every place that the sole of your foot shall tread upon, that have I given unto you, as I said unto Moses. . . . There shall not any man be able to stand before thee all the days of thy life:* **as I was with Moses, so I will be with thee:** *I will not fail thee, nor forsake thee.*

Joshua 1:2–3 and 5

God exalts the humble. When Joshua took over the leadership of Israel, the Lord told Joshua that he would lead the people to conquer the land He had promised them. God promised that He would be with Joshua as He had been with Moses. Later, in Joshua 3:7, the Lord said, *"This day will I begin to magnify thee in the sight of all Israel, that they may know that, as I was with Moses, so I will be with thee."* Because Joshua was humble, God magnified him so that the people would see and respect his leadership.

There was a time in my life when I thought it was wrong to honor a person. I thought all honor had to go directly to God.

Many years ago, Jamie and I were invited to a service honoring a friend of mine who was celebrating forty years of ministry. I was asked to prepare a few words, but I was struggling with what to say. I didn't want to dishonor God by honoring a person. Then the Lord reminded me of the last part of 1 Samuel 2:30. It says, *"Them that honour me I will honour, and they that despise me shall be lightly esteemed."* I realized that there was nothing wrong with honoring someone who had honored the Lord.

That is basically what God said to Joshua when He said He was going to magnify Joshua in the sight of all Israel. God was honoring Joshua for honoring Him by serving Moses. Remember James 4:10? It says, *"Humble yourselves in the sight of the Lord, and he shall lift you up."* It's a law of the kingdom that when you humble yourself, when you become a servant, God lifts you up. He promotes you.

> **❝I realized that there was nothing wrong with honoring someone who had honored the Lord."**

When the Lord told Joshua that He was going to magnify him, it would have been pride for Joshua to respond with, "Oh no, God. I don't want any honor; all honor goes to You. I won't let You magnify me." It would have been prideful to argue with God and refuse to accept the responsibility and honor that goes with the position of God-given leadership.

In 2002, the Lord spoke to my heart and told me it was time for the ministry to expand. We had reached a tipping point. We could either expand into new territory or coast into obscurity—the choice was mine. (You can find the whole story in my teaching *Don't Limit God*.) The Lord wasn't rebuking me for what had been accomplished through the ministry. He was simply letting me know that there was more He wanted to do and that I was limiting Him by my small thinking (Ps. 78:41). I wasn't allowing Him to promote me.

Around this same time, I was invited to be part of a radio show in Tulsa, Oklahoma. Len and Cathy Mink were going to interview me on station KNYD. I'd never met Len and Cathy, but I had known of them for decades. Len led praise and worship for Kenneth Copeland, and the Minks were (at least in my estimation) very influential. I felt a little starstruck going into that interview, but I was flabbergasted when they introduced me. Len began talking about how he'd first heard me years before on radio and how the Lord had impacted him through my ministry. It was overwhelming to think that God had used me to touch a man like Len Mink.

After the interview, we went out to eat. As we sat together, I began expressing how amazed I was that God had used me to touch his life. Len looked at me and said, "You've been on radio for decades. You've been ministering to people all over the United States. Why would it shock you to find that God used you to minister to me?" What he said made sense; I'd just never allowed myself to think that way. I'd not allowed God to honor me. You see, my natural tendencies make it easier for me to fade into the background—to not be on stage—but God has called me to things beyond my ability, things that require humility.

When Joshua led the children of Israel into the battle of Jericho (Josh. 6), he told the people not to take any spoils but to dedicate them as a first-fruits offering to the Lord. The people agreed, but Achan secretly kept a garment and some of the gold and silver for himself (Josh. 7). He hid these things in his tent. Then when the Israelites went to fight their next battle, at Ai, they lost. It didn't make sense. Ai was a tiny town; they should have conquered it easily. Instead, the warriors of Ai killed thirty-six of Israel's fighting men and frightened the rest of the army away.

When Joshua heard what had happened, he fell on his face before the Lord. "Get up," God told Joshua. "Why do you lie on your face? Israel has sinned against Me. They have stolen what was Mine and put it among their own stuff. You're the leader, Joshua. Now deal with this, or I will not be able to use you to take these people into the Promised Land" (Josh. 7:10–12, paraphrase mine).

God chooses leaders who will humble themselves and do what is right. He chooses leaders who will depend on Him. When Joshua learned what Achan had done, he approached Achan and said, *"My son, give glory to the LORD, the God of Israel, and honor him. Tell me what you have done; do not hide it from me"* (Josh. 7:19, NIV). In other words, Joshua told Achan to speak the truth. Speaking the truth glorifies God. But notice what Joshua did not do. He did not concern himself with Achan's response; he simply obeyed God. Joshua was more concerned with honoring God than with appeasing Achan—and those who honor the Lord, God will honor (1 Sam. 2:30).

Chapter Eighteen

HUMILITY GIVES THANKS

Maybe you're thinking, *Okay, Andrew. I get it. Let's move on.* But the things God's Word says about humility need to be shared. Romans 10:17 says, *"Faith cometh by hearing, and hearing by the word of God."* In other words, faith comes when we hear—and hear and hear—the Word. We learn by repetition. And since humility is rarely talked about in our culture or in our churches, we need to keep hearing.

I once heard a story about a preacher who applied for a job to pastor a small church. As part of his interview process, he had to preach to the congregation. He taught on John 3:16. Everyone thought the service was awesome, so they voted him in as pastor. During his first Sunday as pastor, he preached the same message—John 3:16. The people thought it was strange that he'd forgotten what he'd preached to them before, but nobody said anything. The next week he preached John 3:16

"Faith comes when we hear—and hear and hear—the Word." again. The people began to grumble among themselves, saying, "If he does this again, we have to say something." When the pastor preached the same message a fourth time, the people decided they'd had enough. They went to the elders of the church and said, "You've got to talk to the pastor. Surely he knows more than John 3:16."

So, the elders went to the pastor. "Pastor," they said, "you have preached here four times now, and every single sermon has been the exact same thing. We're tired of John 3:16. Don't you know anything else?"

The pastor responded, "When you start living John 3:16, I'll preach something else."

That pastor was very wise. If we would stay with one truth from the Word of God until we truly understood it and began to apply it, I guarantee our lives would change. Unfortunately, most people just crave knowledge. They're not as interested in putting that knowledge to work. That's why I'm spending so much time breaking down humility. God has shown us the way; we just need to do it (Mic. 6:8).

Another of humility's characteristic is thankfulness. Look at this passage in Luke:

> *And it came to pass, as he went to Jerusalem, that he passed through the midst of Samaria and Galilee.*

And as he entered into a certain village, there met him ten men that were lepers, which stood afar off: and they lifted up their voices, and said, Jesus, Master, have mercy on us. And when he saw them, he said unto them, Go shew yourselves unto the priests. And it came to pass, that, as they went, they were cleansed. And one of them, when he saw that he was healed, turned back, and with a loud voice glorified God, and fell down on his face at his feet, giving him thanks: and he was a Samaritan. And Jesus answering said, Were there not ten cleansed? but where are the nine? There are not found that returned to give glory to God, save this stranger. And he said unto him, Arise, go thy way: thy faith hath made thee whole.

Luke 17:11–19

This is the story of Jesus's healing of the ten lepers. The book of Luke describes the event as happening on Jesus's way to Jerusalem, probably for Passover. Here, in a certain village along the border of Samaria and Galilee, Jesus encountered a group of lepers. Most of the people in the group were probably Jews, but Luke identifies at least one as a Samaritan (Luke 17:16).

This is interesting because Jews didn't normally associate with Samaritans. I'm sure their common circumstances erased those typical cultural divisions, at least while they had leprosy.

But notice what happened. When Jesus heard the lepers' cries for mercy, He told them to *"go shew yourselves unto the priests. And it came to pass, that, **as they went**, they were cleansed"* (Luke 17:14). In their humble condition, the lepers believed the words of Jesus. And *"as they went"* to show themselves to the priest—or as they obeyed Jesus's words—they were healed.

But what about the Samaritan? Samaritans weren't part of the covenant people of God. They couldn't count on God's promises. They couldn't worship at the temple or offer sacrifices. They were outsiders, reviled. How was this man to obey Jesus's words? Yet this man, *"when he saw that he was healed, turned back, and with a loud voice glorified God . . . giving him thanks"* (Luke 17:15–16).

Jesus said unto him, *"Were there not ten cleansed? but where are the nine? There are not found that returned to give glory to God, save this stranger"* (Luke 17:17–18). Maybe the Samaritan returned to Jesus because he couldn't go to the temple priests. Maybe he recognized Jesus as *the* High Priest (Heb. 6:20), and instead of bringing Him animal sacrifices the ex-leper brought Jesus a sacrifice of praise (Heb. 13:15). Either way, the Samaritan's thanksgiving gave glory to God (Ps. 50:23). That's what a humble person does.

I struggle to understand the nine lepers who weren't thankful. When Jamie and I get to take a little time off, we often spend it at home, quietly enjoying our relationship with God and one another. Often, I'll just walk around my property, thanking God for the solitude and thanking Him for the beautiful day. And once I start thinking about all God has done, I'm overwhelmed with thankfulness. It humbles me.

I know God doesn't fall off His throne when people don't recognize Him for who He is. I know He doesn't fall into depression when people don't thank Him for His care, but it blesses God when we give Him thanks. The psalmist said that God inhabits the praises of His people (Ps. 22:3). Psalm 100:4 also tells us to *"enter into his gates with thanksgiving, and into his courts with praise."* Paul commanded us to *"rejoice in the Lord always: and again I say, Rejoice"* (Phil. 4:4). Praise belongs to God, and as His people we should be thankful (Ps. 29:2).

During the second phase of the Charis building project in Woodland Park, we ran out of money and I had to temporarily stop construction. During that time, I remember walking through the unfinished Auditorium, thanking God and praising Him for what was already completed. I wasn't discouraged. I knew it would get done, so I thanked Him for the use of The Barn. I thanked Him for a construction crew who was willing to work within our unpredictable schedule. I thanked Him for my partners and for all the money that had come in—over and above our normal expenses—that had enabled the ministry to build. (It takes millions of dollars a month to run our ministry. And at that time, we had spent around $50 million on the Charis project above those regular monthly expenses.)

I can honestly say that as I was walking around and thanking God for what we already had, my faith grew. I remembered all the times God had proven Himself faithful to His Word (1

Thess. 5:24), and I knew He would do it again. I did not experience a single doubt—not one reservation—that I was doing what He had called me to do (Eph. 2:10). I was confident that what He began, He would complete (Phil. 1:6). That's what thanksgiving does. It makes you abound in faith (Col. 2:7).

When you are thankful, when you give glory to God, it puts God in His rightful place as the source of your life. It takes you out of the devil's crosshairs and puts responsibility for the solutions to your problems where it belongs—with God. When the devil comes to accuse you, saying, "What makes you think you can do that?" you can say, "I'm not doing it. God has caused this good to happen. He's the source, and you can't stop Him!" But if you're not a thankful person—if you don't acknowledge God or others, if you're demanding and think people "owe" you respect or gratitude—that's an indication of pride. You may not be arrogant, you may not necessarily think you're better than anyone else, but you are self-centered. You don't view God as your source. You don't recognize the contribution others make in your life, and you need to humble yourself.

> **When you are thankful, when you give glory to God, it puts God in His rightful place as the source of your life."**

I remember praying for a woman crippled with arthritis. She was experiencing a lot of complications tied to the arthritis, and her doctors didn't expect her to live through the week. She was curled up in pain. Her joints were gnarled. She hadn't eaten solid food for nearly eight years. But when I prayed for her, she was instantly healed. She got off her stretcher and started walking back and forth. Within a week, her hands were completely normal, and all other symptoms of arthritis were gone. But, like Jesus and the lepers, I never saw that woman again. She never came to one of my meetings. She never wrote the ministry or called to say thanks. And while her response didn't discourage me from praying for others, her stopping to give thanks would have been the right thing to do.

The sad thing is, many people do this with the Lord. They could be in a life-or-death situation, but when God delivers them, they go right back to what they were doing. They don't stop to thank Him. They don't tell others of His faithfulness. Nothing changes. That's pride.

The book of Hebrews gives us some great instruction regarding thanksgiving:

> *Let us continually offer to God a sacrifice of praise—the fruit of lips that confess his name. And do not forget to do good and to share with others, for with such sacrifices God is pleased.*

Hebrews 13:15–16, NIV

We bless the Lord when we are thankful. But when we think only of ourselves—when we aren't thankful for what God has done or the people He has placed in our lives to minister to

"Practicing thankfulness, whether it's praying for your food or just being polite at the store, is a great habit to get into."

and encourage us—we're proud. We're selfish and self-centered.

Jesus said it's more blessed to give than to receive (Acts 20:35), but a proud person is only concerned with receiving. They only think of their own needs. No one thanks their boss when they get a paycheck. They think, *I earned this*. But I am thankful each time Jamie and I get paid. I remember when we were so poor, we couldn't pay attention. In the early days of the ministry, we nearly starved to death. We went weeks without food when Jamie was eight months pregnant. I remember those days. Just the other day, Jamie was gone and I had to rustle up my own supper. I put a chicken potpie in the microwave and thought of the days we couldn't afford them. I thanked God for His blessings. I thanked God I could go to a restaurant or to the store and buy anything I wanted. That's humility.

Practicing thankfulness, whether it's praying for your food or just being polite at the store, is a great habit to get into. Now, I don't believe we *have* to give thanks for our food. I don't think anyone will go to hell for not being thankful. But thankfulness is one of humility's traits.

Chapter Nineteen

HUMILITY GLORIFIES GOD

The second half of Romans 1—which I teach on in my book *Discover the Keys to Staying Full of God*—is one of the most complete studies in the Bible on the results of pride (Rom. 1:18–32). It explains what happens to a person's heart when they refuse to humble themselves. Right in the middle, it summarizes everything, saying:

> *Because that, when they knew God, they glorified him not as God, neither were thankful; but became vain in their imaginations, and their foolish heart was darkened.*

Romans 1:21

When we aren't humble, when we don't glorify God and practice thankfulness, we are foolish. We allow pride to dig its roots deep into our hearts until our minds become twisted and we can no longer recognize good. We begin taking progressive steps away from God, until we lose all conviction and eventually become reprobate. That's what the rest of this passage in Romans describes, and it all starts with not glorifying and thanking God.

The Greek word translated *glorified* in Romans 1:21 means "to render (or esteem) glorious" (*Strong's Concordance*). To glorify something means you place a high value upon it, or you prize it. Paul used that same Greek word in Romans 11:13 when he said, *"Inasmuch as I am the apostle of the Gentiles, I **magnify** mine office."* In other words, humility glorifies or magnifies—places a high value upon—God.

> **"A humble person will let others get glory without trying to draw attention to their own accomplishments."**

Let's look again at Paul's statement in Romans 11:13: *"For I speak to you Gentiles, inasmuch as I am the apostle of the Gentiles, I magnify mine office."* Some people might find this verse prideful. But I hope you've begun to understand that Paul's statement was not one of pride. He was the apostle of the Gentiles. That's who God called him to be (Acts 9:15), and the Gentiles are the ones the church elders sent him to reach (Gal. 2:7–9). Paul wasn't magnifying himself in this statement; he was magnifying his office—the office God gave him.

I've known many people who magnify self constantly. When someone else earns an honor or accomplishes something, these people interject their own accomplishments into the conversation. They can't stand for others to receive glory when they don't. If the local high school's star football player earned a college scholarship for running the fastest forty-yard dash, this person would comment, "When I was in high school . . ." That's pride. That's seeking glory for oneself. A humble person will let others get glory without trying to draw attention to their own accomplishments.

Whatever we magnify gets bigger. If we magnify self, our selfish motives and desires—with their corresponding emotions—get bigger. But if we magnify the Lord, He gets bigger. Just like we don't actually grow an object by looking at it through a magnifying glass, we can't change the size or importance of God by glorifying Him. God is the same whether we believe and magnify Him or not. God doesn't change; our perception changes (Heb. 13:8 and James 1:17). And just like we can't look through both ends of binoculars at the same time, we cannot glorify God and self at the same time. If we choose to hoard all the glory and credit for our accomplishments, we will, by default, decrease the value—the esteem—we place on God. But if we are truly glorifying God and giving Him thanks, self is automatically diminished.

A great example of this is John the Baptist. John was Jesus's cousin, the son of Elisabeth and Zacharias. He was a miracle baby, dedicated to God from his mother's womb. He lived in the desert until the day he began calling the nation back to God (Luke 3:2–3). His message was so timely and powerful, the people of Israel began to wonder if he was the long-awaited Messiah (Luke 3:15). Luke 3:16 records John's answer to them:

> *I indeed baptize you with water; but one mightier than I cometh, the latchet of whose shoes I am not worthy to unloose: he shall baptize you with the Holy Ghost and with fire.*

John didn't claim to be the Messiah. He didn't promote himself in the eyes of the people. He plainly told them, "I'm not the one." Then one day John saw Jesus coming toward him and shouted, *"Behold the Lamb of God, which taketh away the sin of the world"* (John 1:29), and two of John's own disciples went after Jesus (John 1:35–37).

I don't know many preachers who would do that. Most pastors I know throw a fit if the members of their congregation express interest in another ministry. They criticize and nitpick that ministry in an attempt to discredit it, and they forbid their congregation to attend services at other fellowships, all because of their personal insecurity.

John didn't do that. He wasn't worried about his reputation. He didn't seek to promote himself. As a matter of fact, when the scribes heard that Jesus was also ministering to and baptizing people, they tried to arouse John's jealousy. "Have you heard," they asked, "that Jesus—the one you testified about—is baptizing more people than you have? Everyone is flocking to Him" (John 3:26). But John didn't take the bait. He operated in humility and said:

> *A man can receive nothing, except it be given him*
> *from heaven. Ye yourselves bear me witness, that I*
> *said, I am not the Christ, but that I am sent before*
> *him . . . He must increase, but I must decrease.*
>
> **John 3:27–28 and 30**

John never claimed to be the Christ or Messiah. He was content with the purpose and plan God designed for him. John only wanted to glorify God. If his decrease brought more glory to God, so be it.

I knew of a minister in Colorado Springs, Colorado, who began drawing large numbers of people to his meetings. When a pastor friend of mine saw that this man was doing a better job reaching the people than he was, my friend submitted himself to the man and encouraged his church to do the same. The minister asked my friend to join his staff and help care for the people. I recognize that this is an unusual story, but the church flourished, and both men prospered. They were both more concerned with glorifying God than with glorifying self, and God honored them.

I know of another minister who came to the Colorado Springs area years ago to plant a Full Gospel church. Historically, Colorado Springs did not support Spirit-filled, faith-based churches. At that time, the biggest churches in the area were denominational churches. But this minister's church plant began to prosper, and soon they were looking for a new building. I was with the 400 or so people at the dedication of their new building and was pleased to hear them praise God for His favor and provision. But before the service was over, their praises switched from glorifying God to "Look what we've built!" It was very offensive.

I prophesied to the church out of 1 Samuel 15:17 and 23, where Samuel rebuked Saul for his pride. (*When thou wast little in thine own sight, wast thou not made the head of the tribes of Israel? . . . Because thou hast rejected the word of the LORD, he hath also rejected thee from being king.*) I said, "God has done these things. We need to direct our glory and praise to God, or we could lose His favor just as quickly as we got it." My words were not well received. And before long, the church fell apart. The minister divorced and lost his family, and his administrator went to jail. The minister began selling women's cosmetics to survive. Last I heard, he had passed away.

Brothers and sisters, pride is deadly. It repels the grace of God and leads to destruction. But that doesn't mean we have to run off to a monastery or join a religious faction that mortifies our flesh. Biblical humility does not require that we sleep on the ground or eat only locusts and wild honey. Now, if God called you to do that, obey. But I don't believe living a sterile lifestyle, rejecting all comfort and the good things following God brings, is true humility. In fact, God's Word promises that if we purpose to humble ourselves under His mighty hand, He will exalt us in due time (1 Pet. 5:6). He will honor those who honor Him (1 Sam. 2:30).

A humble person is not a person who never struggles with pride. A humble person is not a person who denies they have to deal with self. A person of humility acknowledges that self exists, but they deny self the preeminent place. Instead, they seek to glorify God and esteem others better than themselves (Phil. 2:3). They choose to be thankful, remembering who God is and all He has done for them. We can't humble ourselves and then refuse God's exaltation and blessing on our lives. Avoiding prosperity because it's "selfish" is not humble. It's not godly. Hebrews 11:6 says:

> *But without faith it is impossible to please him: for he*
> *that cometh to God must believe that he is, and that*
> *he is a rewarder of them that diligently seek him.*

God rewards those who seek Him. It pleases God when He sees His children living in the blessings of humility (Ps. 35:27). If all you're concerned with is the roof over your head, the gas in

❝ In fact, God's Word promises that if we purpose to humble ourselves under His mighty hand, He will exalt us in due time.❞

your car, and the food on your table, you're not humble; you are selfish. True humility says, "I have enough. Now, how can I help others? What can I do to partner with God in establishing His kingdom on the earth?"

> *But thou shalt remember the Lord thy God: for it is he that giveth thee power to get wealth, that he may establish his covenant which he sware unto thy fathers, as it is this day.*
>
> **Deuteronomy 8:18**

Chapter Twenty

HUMILITY DEFUSES ANGER

Angry people are proud people. That may shock you, but it's true. Society often attributes anger to hormones, personality types, or an attempt at personal justification, but that is not what Scripture teaches. Proverbs 13:10 says, *"**Only** by pride cometh contention: but with the well advised is wisdom."* Notice the word *only*. No matter what dictionary or concordance I use to look up that word, it means only. There is no other way for contention or anger to come except by pride. Pride is the root; humility is the solution.

I remember ministering in Pueblo, Colorado over twenty years ago on this very subject. A man came up to me afterward and said, "I respect you. I like your ministry. But you're wrong about anger. I am a very angry person. I have a temper that gets me in trouble all the time. But I am not proud." I'm sure many people feel this way, but it all stems back to our misunderstanding and misapplication of the word *pride*.

Many people think of pride as arrogance. And while arrogance is pride, not all pride presents itself as arrogance. Low self-esteem and insecurity is pride. As I said before, pride is simply self-centeredness. It is focused on self more than God and more than others. At the center of P-R-I-D-E is "I."

I know about this because I was an introvert. I had a hard time talking to anyone who wasn't a family member or close friend. And you know what caused that? Pride. I was thinking only about me. I was worried about what they would think of me. Would I say or do something stupid? That's the root of all shyness and insecurity. When a person is focused on self, that's pride, and according to Scripture, that's where contention is born.

> **" When a person is focused on self, that's pride, and according to Scripture, that's where contention is born."**

I once saw a special on television that was trying to persuade people to eliminate capital punishment from our justice system. They wanted life imprisonment (instead of the death penalty) to become the most severe form of judicial sentencing. Now, I'm not excited about capital punishment, but I do believe it is a biblically sound, sometimes appropriate means of deterring violent crime (Gen. 9:5–6). And I'm pretty firm in that conviction. But as I watched this program, my conviction began to waver.

They did a case study on a man who had raped and murdered a young girl. But instead of focusing on the facts of the case, they began to weave a storyline together that started in this man's childhood. It was emotional. As I watched his baby pictures flash across the television screen, it was difficult to imagine that this innocent child could do anything worthy of death. I watched him grow up playing in the backyard, riding a stick horse, and climbing trees. Then I heard of the abuse he suffered, and I watched this boy turn the corner from victimized child to escalating predator. Then they showed him sitting in his dark cell with his head in his hands. I began to sympathize with this man. Though I knew what he did was wrong, and I felt sorry for the girl's family, I began to pity him. I thought, *Oh God, there are so many extenuating circumstances. Is there not a better way to deal with this man?*

It made me question what I believed. But as I contemplated all this, the Lord spoke to my heart. He said, "Andrew, what if they did a story on the girl this man raped and murdered? What if they showed *her* baby pictures? Showed her playing with dolls and building a snowman? What if they walked you down her high-school halls and showed you her graduation? What if they talked about her fiancé and showed you their engagement photos? What if you knew the plans the two of them had made to marry, buy their first house, and have three children? And what if, in the middle of all that, they told you that some pervert assaulted this woman as she walked to her car, raped her for self-gratification, and then wasn't man enough to face what he'd done, so he killed her to cover up his crime? How would you and the audience feel then?"

I realized that the exact same audience who was mourning our justice system after seeing the man's side of the story would turn into a vigilante committee and string him up from the nearest tree. The Lord spoke again, saying, "It all depends on perspective. Your emotions will respond to either one."

The same is true in any conflict. Our emotions will respond to the perspective we adopt. If we look at our circumstances through a prideful, self-centered perspective, we will get angry. We don't really have a choice. But if we purpose to consider the other person's feelings, the other person's perspective, it will cause sympathy to rise up in our hearts, and we will act mercifully. That's exactly what Proverbs 13:10 is saying. The only thing that causes anger, contention, and strife is pride—looking at things only from a selfish viewpoint.

There were times in my life when my brother nearly beat me to death. He wasn't a terrible person, but he had a terrible temper! Every time he calmed down, he would apologize. "I'm sorry," he'd say. "I didn't realize what I was doing. I wasn't thinking about how I was hurting you. I was only thinking about what you did to me."

That's pride, and the only antidote for it is humility—putting God and others first. Jesus is an amazing example of this concept. If anyone ever had a justification for anger, it was Jesus. He was the sinless Son of God, yet He suffered unjustly. He was mocked and spit upon, stripped and beaten. His beard was ripped out (Is. 50:6). The same people who praised Him in the streets shouted for His crucifixion. But when Jesus hung on the cross, He had compassion on the people. He didn't respond in anger. He could have; He could have called twelve legions of angels to His side and wiped out the entire human race (Matt. 26:53). Instead, He prayed, *"Father, forgive them; for they know not what they do"* (Luke 23:34).

If it's only circumstances that cause a chemical reaction in the brain and trigger a natural response of anger, it would have been impossible for Jesus to respond like that. He would have been angry. Some people think, *That was Jesus. I'm not Jesus; I can't do that.* That's not a good excuse. You may not be Jesus, but you have the same Spirit living in you as Jesus had living in Him (Rom. 8:11). Even Stephen, a man born with a fallen nature and born again by the Spirit of Christ, was able to overcome pain and anger to forgive the very people who were stoning him to death (Acts 7:58–60).

Jesus's and Stephen's actions show that anger is not an uncontrollable, physical reaction. It's a choice. When you're humble, it's impossible to be truly angry and to live life subject to a bad temper. Humility defuses anger. When you esteem others ahead of yourself, you'll be able to pray for those who wrong you, just like Jesus did. That's what humility is all about.

James 4 says:

Speak not evil one of another, brethren. He that speaketh evil of his brother, and judgeth his brother, speaketh evil of the law, and judgeth the law: but if thou judge the law, thou art not a doer of the law, but a judge. There is one lawgiver, who is able to save and to destroy: who art thou that judgest another?

James 4:11–12

We could combine this with Romans 12:19, which says, *"Vengeance is mine; I will repay, saith the Lord."* Humility doesn't speak evil or slander a brother or sister. It doesn't take matters into its own hands and judge in anger or repay evil for evil. Humility submits itself to God and lets God take care of its defense.

Many years ago, I held a meeting in the town of a well-known television minister who was slandering me viciously. I don't know what happened to cause their irrational anger, but one of my staff members attended their church, and since I was in town I thought of attending as well. At the last moment, I changed my mind. Later that afternoon, my staff member told me they had told the people I was

❝ When you're humble, it's impossible to be truly angry and to live life subject to a bad temper. Humility submits itself to God and lets God take care of its defense.❞

the "slickest cult since Jim Jones." They told them to boycott my meetings and burn my materials.

Their words hurt, but I recognized them for what they were—darts of the Enemy. I didn't get angry. I didn't fight back or speak evil of this person. I just kept loving them and supporting their ministry. Twenty years later, this minister and I were being interviewed on the same television program. During a commercial break, they approached me and said, "I love your program! I watch you every day." Since then, we've appeared on numerous programs together and have become friends. I have their number, and they have mine. I've even had them minister at Charis and bless the ministry. I don't know what happened! All I did was refrain from anger, and God defended me.

We have to learn to recognize that people are not the problem (Eph. 6:12). The devil is the one who comes against us. He is the accuser of the brethren (Rev. 12:10). He may use people, but often those people don't realize what they are doing. They may have been having a bad day. Maybe they missed lunch or were up all night with a sick child. Maybe they were simply misinformed. We don't know, and we can't allow ourselves to get angry and retaliate.

I used to travel to a church where the same couple sat on the front row every time I came. They'd get there hours early to get a good seat. I remember prophesying over them once in a very specific way. I mean, it was specific—I either hit the nail on the head, or I was totally in the flesh. The problem was, I didn't get a chance to talk with them afterward to check, and I knew I wouldn't see them until the next time I was in town.

The next time I ministered there, the couple didn't come. Immediately I remembered that prophecy. I figured I must have missed it and offended them. I let my imagination run wild and started picturing them telling everyone I was a false prophet. All that night and the next day, I obsessed over their absence. I got angry, thinking they'd wronged me; I felt like punching something. Then, the next night, they were back on the front row. "We're so sorry," they said when I approached them. "We had a death in the family and couldn't be here yesterday. We would never miss one of your meetings!" I felt like a toad. I had judged them and struggled with hurt feelings for twenty-four hours—and it was completely unfounded! I saw they weren't there, but I didn't know why and jumped to conclusions. Instead of allowing humility to defuse my hurt and anger, I was prideful and took their absence as a personal rejection. It was a powerful lesson to learn!

> **❟❟ Instead of allowing humility to defuse my hurt and anger, I was prideful and took their absence as a personal rejection. It was a powerful lesson to learn!"**

Chapter Twenty-One

JUDGE NOT?

People often misapply the section of Jesus's Sermon on the Mount where He says, *"Judge not, that ye be not judged. For with what judgment ye judge, ye shall be judged: and with what measure ye mete, it shall be measured to you again"* (Matt. 7:1–2). They take these verses to mean that we shouldn't judge anyone or anything. We shouldn't even have an opinion. They use it to say there is no right or wrong, or at least that we shouldn't tell anyone what is right. But this violates Scripture. In another place, Jesus even said, *"Ye hypocrites . . . how is it that ye do not discern this time? Yea, and why even of yourselves judge ye not what is right?"* (Luke 12:56–57).

Jesus never said, "Do not judge." He said, "Do not judge, or you will be judged." In other words, we reap what we sow. Two of the seven pastors of Asia were rebuked by the Lord because they didn't judge the people who were teaching error in their churches (Rev. 2:14–16, 20–23). The apostle Paul said in 1 Corinthians 5:3 that he judged and in 1 Corinthians 10:13

> *"Jesus never said, 'Do not judge.' He said, 'Do not judge, or you will be judged.' In other words, we reap what we sow."*

he told the Corinthians to judge what he said.

The bottom line is, we have to judge. We make judgments every day about the weather. We judge the price of this pair of shoes compared with that pair. We judge whether we have enough time to get through a yellow stoplight safely. There's nothing wrong with judgments. It is wise to judge whether or not you can trust someone. It is wise to judge who should have access to your financial records or who would try to steal from you. Jesus didn't warn us against making judgments. He warned us against judging in a way that we don't want to be judged. He warned us against making unjust judgments.

> *Judge not according to the appearance, but judge righteous judgment.*
>
> ### John 7:24

Have you ever heard the old saying "Don't judge a book by its cover"? I'm pretty sure it came from this verse. We shouldn't judge people or situations rashly. We should not judge based on outward appearance. We need to get the facts. And we need to extend mercy to others until we can make a "righteous judgment."

A woman once came to me complaining about her pastor. Apparently, she was used to the pastor greeting her each Sunday morning, but one particular morning he didn't. "He's angry at me," this woman said. "He walked right past me and didn't even acknowledge me. Even when I tried to greet him, he just kept his head down and moved on. I'm not sure I want to go to a church where I'm invisible." She started blasting her pastor and attributing blame to him, until I interrupted. "How do you know he rejected you?" I said. "Maybe he had to go to the bathroom. Maybe he had to deal with a problem among his staff. Maybe he got called to the hospital the night before and didn't get home until three o'clock in the morning. Maybe he realized he forgot to brush his teeth. Maybe God was speaking to him about his sermon. You aren't the center of the universe. Is it possible that he had his mind on something besides you? I don't know what happened, but neither do you. Don't make an unrighteous judgment against him."

You know, one of the qualifications of an elder is sober-mindedness (1 Tim. 3:2). That word *sober* isn't talking about not being drunk. It basically means to be void of speculative imagination. We shouldn't speculate about people's motives. We don't need to imagine we understand why people do what they do. It would not have been wrong for that lady to go to her pastor and ask, "Pastor, is something wrong? I walked by this morning and said hello, but you didn't respond." There's nothing wrong with that. The problem lies in assigning blame and assuming motivation. She didn't know what was in her pastor's heart or mind; she didn't have all the facts. And because of it, she couldn't make a righteous judgment.

When Peter and John were arrested and told they could not preach anymore in the name of Jesus, they answered, "Judge for yourself whether it is right in God's sight to obey Him or obey you" (Acts 4:19, paraphrase mine). Yet society says, "Only the Supreme Court has the right to judge. If the Supreme Court says homosexual marriage or abortion is okay, everyone else must agree. Christians can't judge someone's sin or morality."

Christians aren't judging sin. They aren't judging whether homosexuality (or any other sin) is wrong. God already judged that. It is wrong. Christians are simply choosing to agree with God. In humility, they are judging righteously.

In Matthew 7:3–5, Jesus continued His sermon about judging:

> *And why beholdest thou the mote that is in thy brother's eye, but considerest not the beam that is in thine own eye? Or how wilt thou say to thy brother, Let me pull out the mote out of thine eye; and, behold, a beam is in thine own eye? Thou hypocrite, first cast out the beam out of thine own eye; and then shalt thou see clearly to cast out the mote out of thy brother's eye.*

Again, this isn't saying we should never judge. We have to be able to make right judgments, but we should also make merciful judgments. We shouldn't judge based on appearance or surface facts. We shouldn't judge from our viewpoint only or critique others' problems when we struggle with the same issues. That's pride. We need to judge ourselves before we judge others so we can extend mercy.

You know, people see things differently. We think differently. Different things are important to us. That's not to say those differences are wrong or that someone else's viewpoint isn't valid; it can just make disagreements difficult to work through.

For example, there was a man on my ministry team who always seemed to disagree with me. If I said, "Go east," he would say, "No, we've got to go west." One day, in the middle of one of those instances, I nearly lost it. I nearly accused him of not being a team player, of setting himself against me. But I caught myself. I knew what I was thinking wasn't true; it just felt like that in the heat of the moment. As a matter of fact, the more I thought about it, the more I realized his different viewpoint actually made our team stronger. It forced us to think deeper, to make well-rounded decisions that would benefit the ministry long term.

The point I'm making is we all have to learn to work through disagreements. We all have to learn to handle uncomfortable situations. Part of humility is learning to do that in an unselfish way. It's not wrong to go to someone and say, "I didn't like what you did (or said) here. Can you explain this to me?" It is wrong to go to someone in anger and judge his or her motivations. It is wrong to slander them and spread rumors about the situation in an attempt to get others to agree with you. That's not beneficial. The Bible tells us to go to a fellow believer alone (Matt. 18:15), not to chew them out, not to demand an apology or avenge ourselves, but with the goal of reconciliation (Matt. 5:24).

I was being interviewed for a radio program once about this process of forgiveness and reconciliation, and I gave an example of a woman I'd ministered to who had been in an abusive relationship. Her husband had beaten her and the kids and threatened to kill them. She came to me for prayer and counsel, and I encouraged her to start praying for him. After a time, the Lord began working in her heart to forgive her husband and reconcile with him. The Lord gave her a special love for her husband and began showing her why her husband was abusive.

As I was telling this story, the interviewer stopped me and said, "We can't use this. I can't put this story on air and encourage people to stay in abusive relationships. Someone might get killed."

"You do what you want," I said. "I'm not advocating that everyone stay in an abusive relationship. I'm just telling you how this woman survived a terrible situation and saw God turn things around."

Because this woman humbled herself and quit looking at things from only her perspective, she was able to forgive her husband. She realized that hurt people hurt people, and as she demonstrated Christ's love to him, her husband was born again. Their marriage was restored.

Now, I don't want you to get discouraged if reconciliation doesn't immediately happen in your situation. You might do everything right, but you can't control how another person will respond to you. Remember, the humble cast their care upon the Lord (1 Pet. 5:6–7). In situations where you've done your best but things just aren't working out, all you can do is submit yourself to God and trust Him to deal with it. You can't force people to change. You can't use your faith to eliminate opposition or force others to receive you.

I actually know people who try to use their authority as a believer to remove all resistance from their life. They get up in the morning and rebuke the devil. They declare that everyone will love them and that all opposition will get out of their way. They're wasting time. Paul said, *"Yea, and all that will live godly in Christ Jesus shall suffer persecution"* (2 Tim. 3:12). We live in a fallen world. Circumstances will come against us. People will persecute and criticize us. It's part of living godly.

> **❝ In situations where you've done your best but things just aren't working out, all you can do is submit yourself to God and trust Him to deal with it.❞**

When someone criticizes you for speaking the truth or preaching the Gospel, it's generally because you hit a nerve. They retaliate to avoid conviction. People get mad at me all the time. When I say it's been decades since I've been discouraged, they come out of the woodwork. I guess my testimony convicts them. They rail at me and call me a liar. "Everyone gets discouraged," they say. "You can't say you've never been discouraged."

I'm not saying I haven't had discouraging things happen to me, but God has supernaturally kept me encouraged. When I tell people I haven't been discouraged, I'm actually trying to encourage them. I'm trying to tell them they don't have to live on an emotional roller coaster—God has something better. Emotional highs and lows are not a normal part of life. I understand many people experience them, but Isaiah said Jesus would exalt every valley and level every mountain (Is. 40:4). That doesn't mean there aren't problems, but Jesus's work in our hearts should make things better and smooth things out.

When people live in rebellion to God's ways rather than humble themselves and repent, it's easier to discredit the messenger. It's like a court trial. When someone gives damaging testimony in court, the first thing a defendant's lawyer tries to do is discredit the witness. They pull skeletons out of a witness's background. They try to confuse the witness so he or she will perjure themselves. They do whatever they can to discredit the witness and get their testimony thrown out. It's not personal. They're just

> **That doesn't mean there aren't problems, but Jesus's work in our hearts should make things better and smooth things out."**

defending their client. Likewise, when someone testifies to the truth of the Word, Satan's first line of defense is to attack the witness. If he can discredit the witness and get the messenger to respond in anger, it puts their testimony into question. But if a witness humbles self and continues to walk in love, the power of their testimony increases.

Chapter Twenty-Two

HUMILITY IS MERCIFUL

God is merciful. He is not the author of the problems and tragedies we face in life. He is not guilty of killing our kids. He is not guilty of causing natural disasters. He doesn't sovereignly choose who will be poor, who will be sick, and who will believe. Those issues stem from sin in general and our own foolish decisions. But religious people don't like to hear this. It's easier to cast blame onto some far-off ruler of the cosmos than to look a little closer to home. The "God card" either gives them an alibi or brings them a measure of comfort. It gives "reason" to the pain they experience.

I know of a man who lost his sister as a child. The two of them were extremely close, and the church, trying to comfort the family, wrongly told them that God had taken the little girl. This little boy determined in his heart that if God did exist, he hated Him. That little boy went on to build a media empire that openly opposes God and everyone who represents Him.

As believers, when we respond to people emotionally or we flippantly play the God card to answer tough questions, we run the risk of misrepresenting God. Our pride sets in motion a series of unintended, far-reaching consequences. We make selfish decisions. We hurt others. We destroy trust and ruin relationships.

Many times throughout my ministry, I've heard or read stories similar to that media mogul's. And when someone like that comes out against me, I think, *What have they experienced in life to cause such hatred and anger and bitterness?* Because I humble myself and don't take their words or actions personally, I've been able to penetrate their pain and minister to many of them.

Humility keeps you from getting angry. It reminds you of all the mercy God has shown you, and it helps you show that mercy to others. Jesus told a story of a servant who owed his master an exorbitant amount of money. When his master called him for an accounting, the servant couldn't pay. He begged his master for mercy, saying, "Lord, have patience with me, and I will pay thee all." The master was merciful. He forgave the man his debt and let him go (Matt. 18:23–27).

❛❛ It reminds you of all the mercy God has shown you, and it helps you show that mercy to others."

Jesus said this same man then left his master and found a fellow servant who owed him a few dollars. The man threatened the fellow servant who owed him money and demanded to be repaid. The servant fell at his feet and begged for mercy, but the man wouldn't give it. He threw his fellow servant into prison until the debt was paid (Matt. 18:28–30). When the master heard of his servant's behavior, he called for the man to appear before him.

> *Then his lord, after that he had called him, said unto him, O thou wicked servant, I forgave thee all that debt, because thou desiredst me: shouldest not thou also have had compassion on thy fellowservant, even as I had pity on thee? And his lord was wroth, and delivered him to the tormentors, till he should pay all that was due unto him.*
>
> **Matthew 18:32–34**

Though this man was shown mercy, he refused to give mercy. He was proud and selfish. He enjoyed the personal results of his master's mercy, but he didn't allow that mercy to change his heart. That man was like a lot of Christians. But notice what Jesus said: *"So likewise shall my heavenly Father do also unto you, if ye from your hearts forgive not every one his brother their trespasses"* (Matt. 18:35).

God has forgiven us a huge debt! If we truly understood how much mercy and grace we've been shown, it would cause us to be gracious and merciful to others. People who are unforgiving and harsh—who demand what they aren't willing to give—don't really understand how much God has forgiven them.

Claiming that your attitude or the way you treat others is a personality trait or part of your "gifting" is a carnal cop-out. You can be straightforward without being harsh. You can learn to speak the truth from a motivation of love (Eph. 4:15). Scripture says we must die to self to become a true follower of Christ (Luke 9:23–24).

What happens when you insult a corpse? Nothing. You can ignore that corpse, cuss it out, spit on it, kick it, and that corpse will just lie there. It won't respond. Why? Because it's dead. If you're struggling to respond to people with mercy and grace, it's because you've not died to self. Your self is still very much alive. If you were to humble yourself, look at the big picture, and put God and His kingdom ahead of your personal agenda, it wouldn't matter so much what happened to you. If someone criticized and lied about you, ruining your career, you could still respond in mercy.

Jesus said:

> *Wherefore I say unto thee, Her sins, which are many, are forgiven; for she loved much: but to whom little is forgiven, the same loveth little.*

Luke 7:47

In this verse, Jesus was talking about the woman who was taken in the act of adultery. The Pharisees wanted to stone her, but Jesus was merciful (John 8:2–11). When she heard that Jesus had returned to her village and was

> **If you're struggling to respond to people with mercy and grace, it's because you've not died to self."**

eating at a Pharisee's house, she came and fell at His feet. She wept over them, dried them with her hair, and anointed them with perfume. The Pharisee criticized Jesus, thinking He didn't know who the woman was. Jesus said, "Because this woman has been forgiven much, she loves much."

I remember counseling a husband and wife who were struggling to love. The woman, who was a Christian, complained that her husband was harsh and bitter—an angry man. She wanted me to condemn him and justify her bad attitude. But instead, I looked at her and said, "He can't give you what he hasn't got. You expect him to be kind to you, to operate in love and mercy, but he's never received kindness, love, or mercy. He doesn't know how much God loves him, and you've not shown him the truth." Then I turned to the man and began sharing the love of God with him. Once he understood God's love, he was able to receive it and give it to his wife.

We can't give away what we don't have. Most of us don't understand how much God loves us, how much He's forgiven us. Love is the antithesis of pride. Jesus said the greatest demonstration of love is a person laying down their life for another (John 15:13). That's what He did for us. And that's what—as children of God—He's asked us to do for others. We are to reflect God's character by laying down our lives, our good, our advancement for the sake of another.

I've said this before, but humility is a process. It's not something anyone comes by naturally. By nature, we are selfish. When a little baby is hungry, they cry. They don't care if everyone else in the house is sleeping. When their diaper needs changing, they don't care if their mother has been up all night and is sleepy. When that baby gets bored in church, they don't care if everyone else is trying to receive from God; if they want attention, they throw a fit. Babies are selfish. They are the center of their universe. And that's okay for a baby.

❙❙ Love is the antithesis of pride. Jesus said the greatest demonstration of love is a person laying down their life for another."

The problem lies in thirty- or forty-year-olds still carrying that same attitude—especially when they are born again.

Once we're born again, that fallen human nature of selfishness is replaced with God's nature of humility (2 Cor. 5:17). Our job as Christians is to learn about this new nature and to renew our minds to who we are in Christ (Rom. 12:2). The easiest way to do that is to look at Jesus. Our new nature is identical to His. First John 4:17 says, *"As he is, so are we in this world."* Right now, the fullness of the Godhead lives in us (Col. 2:9–10). Like God, we are full of love, joy, peace, long-suffering, gentleness, goodness, faith, meekness, and temperance (Gal. 5:22–23). It's who we are, but we have to renew our minds to this truth to experience the benefits.

A parent's most important job is to teach their children that the world does not revolve around them, that life is not all about getting what the child wants. But not all parents do what's best for their children. Many parents just do what is easiest. Have you ever seen a child throw a fit in the grocery store? Maybe they want a piece of candy or a toy, and their mother says no. The child screams and throws him- or herself on the floor to get what they want. Embarrassed, the mother gives in. She buys what her child wants and, in so doing, reinforces their selfishness.

Society reinforces selfishness. There are a lot of thirty-, forty-, and fifty-year-olds having temper tantrums every day in our society. The tantrums may be more sophisticated than a child throwing him- or herself on the floor, but they are temper tantrums just the same. God has called us to live differently. He has called us to be *"conformed to the image of his Son"* (Rom. 8:29). And as painful as it can be to put others ahead of self, to lay down our grievances for the sake of mercy, doing so pleases God. It is a tangible expression of the love of Christ.

.

Chapter Twenty-Three

A DAILY COMMITMENT

Humility is a spiritual process. It takes effort and commitment. It takes a daily (sometimes moment-by-moment) sacrificing of self. Paul wrote:

> *I beseech you therefore, brethren, by the mercies of God, that ye present your bodies a living sacrifice, holy, acceptable unto God, which is your reasonable service.*

Romans 12:1

Paul wrote this to believers—not pastors, not missionaries, but *all* believers. It doesn't matter if God calls you into business or health care. It doesn't matter if you're called to be a mother or a full-time minister. We all have different vocational callings, but God called each of us—regardless of age—to become a

We all have different vocational callings, but God called each of us—regardless of age—to become a living sacrifice.

living sacrifice. That is our *reasonable service*" or our normal Christian duty. This isn't for the super saint. This is for every Jane- and John-Doe Christian out there.

You're never going to live perfectly humble, but you can start heading in that direction.

While I was in Vietnam, the United States sent its first man to the moon. I was disappointed to miss the television specials and interviews, so when I got back, I looked for every piece of information about the Apollo missions I could find. Later I ended up on the same television program as James "Jim" Irwin. Jim Irwin walked on the moon in 1971. He devoted his life to Christ after his experience in space, and he wrote a book about his voyage and what it meant to him spiritually.

During the television program, Jim and I exchanged books, and I started pumping him for information. I wanted to know how the rocket worked and if the mission went exactly as planned. I had this idea that with all the technology NASA had, everything went perfectly. But that's not what happened. Jim explained that NASA basically threw their capsule toward the moon, and for four and a half days, they course-corrected every ten minutes. He said sometimes the moon was right in front of them, and they didn't have to make much of a correction. Other times they would find themselves traveling perpendicular to the moon, and they'd have to execute a huge space maneuver to get back in line. The capsule's journey to the moon was far from perfect!

Jim also told me that his crew had a targeted landing strip on the moon of 500 miles. When they landed and got out of the lunar module, he said they were within five feet of missing that target! As he was explaining these things to me, I realized that just like they had to have a course correction every ten minutes, we have to course-correct in our walk of humility—sometimes every ten minutes!

You know, the Lord really started this process in me on March 23, 1968. That night, when I recognized my selfishness and choose to humble myself before the Lord, I blasted off and headed toward the moon. But I have had a million course corrections since then! Those course corrections don't mean I didn't make a real commitment to humility. I did. But I still have to deal with self every day. I still have to choose to put others first and look at things from their perspective. It's an ongoing process. I may fail in my motivation or dedication to that commitment, but that just means I'm human. When I fail, I simply repent and make a course correction (1 John 1:9).

It's kind of like dieting. People who struggle with weight get on these extreme diets and punish themselves for a brief period of time. They see results, but once the diet is over, they return to their old eating habits and find themselves right back where they started. Some actually gain more weight after dieting. To really control weight, a person has to learn to manage their eating and exercise habits for the rest of their life, not just for a few weeks. The same is true of becoming a living sacrifice. We can't just humble ourselves once and be done with it. Humility is a lifestyle.

Paul continued his letter to the Romans, saying:

> *And be not conformed to this world: but be ye transformed by the renewing of your mind, that ye may prove what is that good, and acceptable, and perfect, will of God.*

Romans 12:2

When we become a living sacrifice and begin the process of renewing our minds, Paul said we *"prove what is that good, and acceptable, and perfect, will of God."* It happens in stages. We grow. We don't go from the earth to the moon overnight, just like we can't go from zero to a thousand miles an hour all at once. That's not acceleration; it's a wreck!

On March 23, 1968, if the Lord had shown me everything I needed to overcome throughout my entire life—all of my wrong attitudes, all the times I would have to practice humility—it would have overwhelmed me. I don't think I could have handled it. I would've probably given up. But praise God, He is merciful and only shows us things a step at a time!

Humility is a vital part of walking intimately with the Lord (Mic. 6:8 and Amos 3:3). You cannot really walk with God and enjoy the kind of life God wants for you while operating in pride. Paul said, *"For though I would desire to glory* [or boast], *I shall not be a fool"* (2 Cor. 12:6). In Scripture, a fool is synonymous with a person who doesn't believe or trust in God. Twice David said, *"The fool hath said in his heart, There is no God"* (Ps. 14:1 and 53:1). So, when Paul said he was not going to be a fool, he was saying, "I'm not going to talk or act like a lost man. I'm not going to speak and boast like someone who doesn't know God."

When the scribes and Pharisees struggled to believe Jesus, He asked, *"How can ye believe, which receive honour one of another, and seek not the honour that cometh from God only?"* (John 5:44). In other words, it's impossible to believe when we esteem man's opinion and approval of greater worth than God's. Don't get me wrong. We need to love others. We need to develop positive relationships with them so we can be a blessing. But we also have to come to a place of commitment that says, "If God says it, I will do it. It doesn't matter if anyone else understands or approves."

> *You cannot really walk with God and enjoy the kind of life God wants for you while operating in pride.*

Let's look at the verses surrounding Jesus's statement to the Pharisees. They had been criticizing Him, saying, "By what authority do You do these miracles? And who gave You this authority?" And Jesus said:

Search the scriptures; for in them ye think ye have eternal life: and they are they which testify of me. And ye will not come to me, that ye might have life. I receive not honour from men. But I know you, that ye have not the love of God in you. I am come in my Father's name, and ye receive me not: if another shall come in his own name, him ye will receive. How can ye believe, which receive honour one of another, and seek not the honour that cometh from God only?

John 5:39–44

Man-pleasers are not people of faith, and they should not expect to receive the benefits of God's grace. Humility is a large part of faith. It is the laying down of self—the setting aside of personal agenda and promotion, personal philosophy and dependence—and the exaltation—the dependence on, the trusting in and glorifying—of God and His Word. We cannot operate in Bible faith when we are seeking the honor and approval of man. This doesn't mean God expects any of us to be perfect. He's just looking for those whose hearts are fully committed to Him.

For the eyes of the LORD range throughout the earth to strengthen [or give grace to] *those whose hearts are fully committed to him.*

2 Chronicles 16:9a, NIV

Paul, arguably the most influential of the apostles and the man God used to write nearly half the books in the New Testament, said he *"would desire to glory"* (2 Cor. 12:6). As humble as Paul was, as much grace as he had received, he still had to deal with pride and selfish ambition. He still had the carnal desire to glory in self, but he refused to give in to it and be a fool. Brothers and sisters, as long as we live in a body of flesh, we will be tempted to shift toward self and pride. We will always be making course corrections. But our commitment to the Lord—our commitment to humility—must not waver.

As you've been reading this book, maybe you've realized that you've never offered your body as a living sacrifice to God. Maybe what you've read has challenged you, causing you to think differently about humility and pride. Maybe you've realized how selfish your life has been, why you've struggled to find promotion and favor. If so, it's time to blast off. It's time to start moving in the right direction.

You can pray right now:

> *Father God, I present myself to You today as a living sacrifice. I know I can't overcome self on my own, so I crawl up on the altar and ask that You consume me—consume this self—like You consumed the sacrifices of old. Show me how much You love me, how much You've forgiven me, so I can love and forgive others. I humble myself. I put You first. I will trust and obey Your Word. Help me*

now to see others as You see them, to put their needs ahead of my own. Thank You for the power of the Holy Spirit to teach me Your ways and help me live out my commitment. In Jesus's name.

Amen! You know, committing to walk in humility is like standing in a mud puddle. Each time you try to clean one foot, the other one gets dirty. You need someone to hold you up out of the mud so you can clean both feet off at the same time. Likewise, when you commit to dying to self, you only start the process. You may pull into the parking lot tomorrow and get cut off. Someone may accuse you of being a radical at work. Your child may throw a fit while you're waiting in line at the bank. You need the Holy Spirit to empower you in those moments to live out your commitment to love God and put others ahead of self. Without Him, it is impossible. You will get frustrated. You will feel embarrassed. But God is faithful; the Holy Spirit is with you. He will be your Helper and make all things possible (John 14:26 and Matt. 19:26).

> **❝I humble myself. I put You first. I will trust and obey Your Word. Help me now to see others as You see them, to put their needs ahead of my own.❞**

Chapter Twenty-Four

HUMILITY
AND FAITH

One time, a woman wrote in to the ministry about our policy of free teaching materials. She said, "I know you give your tapes away free of charge, but I don't want anything free. I pay my own way. Please send me three tapes and a bill." We sent her the requested tapes, but we didn't send a bill. She wrote back to us, "I enjoyed those tapes, but you didn't send me a bill. I want to order three more tapes. Add the cost to my original bill and send the bill with the tapes. I pay my own way." So, we sent her three more tapes and no bill. She wrote in again, this time irate: "I am not a freeloader! I pay my own way. Send me a bill for my tapes, or I will never contact this ministry again!"

So, I sent her a personal tape addressing her concern. I told her, "I don't put a price on my teachings. They are worth more money than you've got. We make suggested donation amounts people can send, but I'm not going to sell you my material or send you a bill. Please receive it as a gift. If it blesses you and you want to send a gift to bless the ministry, we'll receive it. But you cannot pay for this material." I don't think we ever heard back from that lady. But that is how gifting works. You don't purchase gifts, and you can't earn them. They are given free of charge or obligation.

God's grace is a gift. He has provided everything for us without charge or obligation. But it's up to us to humble ourselves and receive His gift by faith. That's really what faith is—humility. Any person who comes to God saying "I've done this, and now You have to respond to me" is in pride. God resists the proud; He gives His gift of grace to the humble (James 4:6).

> **❝ You don't purchase gifts, and you can't earn them. They are given free of charge or obligation.❞**

I don't think I've ever heard someone make this connection between faith and humility, but a number of scriptures link the two. For instance, Romans 5:2 says, *"By whom also we have access by faith into this grace wherein we stand, and rejoice in hope of the glory of God."* We access grace by faith, by humility.

The book of Romans is Paul's masterpiece on the subject of grace. In the first four chapters, Paul described what it means to have faith in God. Then he used the examples of Abraham and David to illustrate how faith works in relation to grace. He showed us that Abraham wasn't perfect, but because he believed God, God counted his faith as righteousness (Gen. 15:6 and Rom. 4:3). Abraham didn't deserve all that God did in his life. It was a gift of grace. Paul then described David's life in terms of his faith, his failure, and God's grace. Paul echoed David's sentiments from Psalm 32:2, saying, *"Blessed is the man to whom the Lord will not impute sin"* (Rom. 4:8). And that's where Paul laid out this huge statement in Romans 5:2:

> *By whom also we have access by faith into this grace wherein we stand, and rejoice in hope of the glory of God.*

The Greek word translated *access* here literally means "admission" (*Strong's Concordance*). For example, seeing a movie at the theatre requires an admission ticket, a payment. Our admission into grace requires the "payment" of faith. Put that together with James's statement that God gives grace to the humble (James 4:6), and we see how it all ties together. True humility is putting faith in God, and true faith is humbly responding to Him. Too many people try to earn the grace of God, but grace only comes when we choose to humble ourselves in faith. We can't earn it. God's grace is not dependent on our goodness. It's not dependent on our church attendance or tithing record. God's grace depends only on humility. We must humble ourselves and look beyond our performance— beyond our failure—to trust and put faith in His grace.

People often tell me, "I know God heals. I know it's His will to heal me. But I don't see it. I don't understand. I live holy. I've confessed the Word. I go to church. I pay my tithes. Why hasn't God healed me?" And I have to tell them, "You're not healed because you're trusting in your own righteousness. You just pointed to all the things you're doing to please God; you never mentioned what Jesus did. You think if you confess the Word 500 times and do steps 1–5, God will be obligated to move. That's not faith. That's coercion. That's pride. You receive God's grace as a gift."

I've also heard people say things like, "Look at this car God gave me! I believed for it. I exercised my faith for a month, and *boom!*" They may say God was the ultimate source, but if you listen, they really believe their works and confession of faith got them a car. Now, don't get me wrong. I believe in faith. I believe we need to confess our faith. I believe that faith is voice activated. But true faith isn't prideful.

I once met a man who beat himself as penance for his sins. He showed me his hands, arms, and knees covered in scars. Where he was from, it was common in the Catholic Church for a person to humiliate their body the week before Easter. Some gave up meat, and others were whipped. Some even offered themselves to be crucified. This man said his scars came from crawling three miles on his hands and knees over pieces of broken glass.

Those things are offensive to God! They're evidence of pride. Though those people may mean well, they are diminishing the work Jesus did for them on the cross. They think their sacrifice will spur God's compassion and make Him accept them. A truly humble attitude would say, "God, I can't do anything to atone for my sins. Thank You for sending Jesus to do what I could not. I humble myself and receive Your grace by faith."

Paul wrote:

> *But now the righteousness of God without the law is manifested, being witnessed by the law and the prophets; even the righteousness of God which is by faith of Jesus Christ unto all and upon all them that believe: for there is no difference: for all have sinned, and come short of the glory of God; being justified freely by his grace through the redemption that is in Christ Jesus.*
>
> **Romans 3:21–24**

Then notice what he said in verse 27:

> *Where is boasting then? It is excluded. By what law? of works? Nay: but by the law of faith.*

True faith eliminates boasting. Bible faith is humble. It excludes pride. It is completely dependent on God and gives Him all glory. It doesn't try to take or earn glory for self. People who do penance—whether by inflicting their body with

❝They take pride in their holiness and pain, and they approach God with an attitude of 'You owe me.'❞ pain or completing their laundry list of Christian "duties"—become proud. They take pride in their holiness and pain, and they approach God with an attitude of "You owe me." Then when their prayers aren't answered, they get mad at God. They feel like God let them down.

I've seen people destroy their faith in the middle of a miracle healing service. God is moving. People are being healed. Blind eyes are seeing and deaf ears are opening. But instead of rejoicing, some people grumble to themselves, *I want a word from God. I want a touch from God. Why can't I receive? How come God is moving in other people's lives and not mine?* Their selfishness repels the grace of God, and they leave those services frustrated instead of encouraged.

But humility takes a different view of the situation—like it's next in line at the bank. When you go to the bank to withdraw money, you don't get upset when the person in line ahead of you finalizes his or her transaction first. You know there is still money in the bank. You just think, *I'm next.*

The same is true for God's grace; there is plenty on deposit for you. So, don't get upset when someone else makes a withdrawal. Humble yourself. Rejoice with those who rejoice (Rom. 12:15), and praise God that you're next in line! That's Bible faith.

Faith doesn't move God. God is not the one who's stuck! God moved on our behalf 2,000 years ago. Through Jesus, He provided salvation, healing, peace, deliverance, and provision for the whole world. It's done. Now we must choose to either believe and receive that provision as a gift, or doubt and do without. Faith doesn't move God; Bible faith moves us. It moves us to humble self and respond to God.

❝ When you go to the bank to withdraw money, you don't get upset when the person in line ahead of you finalizes his or her transaction first. You know there is still money in the bank. You just think, I'm next.❞

Whether you've found yourself wallowing in self-pity or swimming in self-righteousness, you have to get beyond it and humble yourself for your faith to work. Pray this prayer:

Father, I humble myself. I will not let what I've done overshadow what You did. Your sacrifice is infinitely greater than my sin, Your righteousness infinitely better. I forget myself. Like Paul, I count my deeds, both good and bad, as dung (Phil. 3:8) and focus on Christ. I know I am not worthy of Your grace, but I humble myself now and receive it. Amen.

Chapter Twenty-Five

HUMILITY IS CONSISTENT

Toward the end of the apostle Paul's ministry, the Lord called him to Jerusalem. On his way, Paul stopped in Miletus (a city in Greece) and called for the elders of the church at Ephesus to meet him there. By this time, the church at Ephesus may have included as many as 100,000 believers who met in homes throughout the city. Each home would have had an elder who cared for the people and answered to Timothy. All those leaders—perhaps hundreds of them—met Paul in Greece. It was, in a sense, the first ministers' conference.

Paul began encouraging the ministers, saying:

> *Ye know, from the first day that I came into Asia, after what manner I have been with you at all seasons, serving the Lord with all humility of mind, and with many tears, and temptations, which*

befell me by the lying in wait of the Jews: and how
I kept back nothing that was profitable unto you,
but have shewed you, and have taught you pub-
lickly, and from house to house, testifying both to
the Jews, and also to the Greeks, repentance toward
God, and faith toward our Lord Jesus Christ.

Acts 20:18b–21

Some may view this statement as one of pride, but Paul wasn't exalting himself. He specifically referenced his humility (Acts 20:19). He was encouraging these leaders to follow his example in following Christ (1 Cor. 11:1). Paul was not asking them to be perfect. He said in Philippians, *"I count not myself to have apprehended: but this one thing I do . . . I press toward the mark for the prize of the high calling of God in Christ Jesus"* (Phil. 3:13–14). Paul wasn't perfect, but he kept going. He held on to the faith (2 Tim. 4:7). He was consistent. So, Paul used this opportunity to encourage these leaders to do the same. He wanted them to continue serving the Lord with *"all humility of mind,"* always in submission to and dependent upon God, giving Him glory but never denying how He used them.

Paul knew he was leaving these men and heading into a hotbed of persecution (Acts 20:22–23). Jerusalem was the seat of Jewish legalism at this time; they hated the message of Christ there. The Jews had killed Jesus's brother, James. They'd imprisoned Peter, and the remaining disciples were scattered abroad, preaching the Gospel everywhere they went. In Paul's mind, it was probable that he would never see these men again (Acts 20:25). That is why he said, *"I've kept nothing back that was profitable to you"* (Acts 20:20). Paul had declared the whole counsel of God to these men. He was confident that if they held on to humble faith, they would succeed in leading the church without him.

I think it is important that we understand how humble Paul was at this moment. Most people would not have continued toward Jerusalem knowing that prison and suffering awaited them. Most people won't put themselves into situations where they know they'll be hated; they won't speak the truth when that truth will get them imprisoned. But Paul knew such things were coming. Still, he went. *"None of these things move me,"* he said (Acts 20:24). Paul was committed to serving God

> **❝ Most people won't put themselves into situations where they know they'll be hated; they won't speak the truth when that truth will get them imprisoned. But Paul knew such things were coming."**

regardless of his own personal welfare. If serving God meant he would be slandered, thrown into prison, whipped and beaten with rods, or stoned and left for dead, Paul was willing to endure it. He had died to self.

But none of these things move me, neither count I my life dear unto myself, so that I might finish

*my course with joy, and the ministry, which I have
received of the Lord Jesus, to testify the gospel of the
grace of God.*

Acts 20:24

Wow.

A humble person doesn't count their life as *"dear unto"* themselves. Now, don't misunderstand. This does not mean we should abuse or mistreat our bodies. We are the temple of the Lord and should be taking care of our bodies (1 Cor. 6:19). There is balance to what I'm saying. But we should not love self to the degree that our faith is shaken or moved by potential suffering. We need to love the truth. We need to love our neighbors so much that we willingly speak the truth in love regardless of the consequences. It's the truth that sets people free (John 8:32).

❞ We need to love the truth. We need to love our neighbors so much that we willingly speak the truth in love regardless of the consequences. It's the truth that sets people free."

Paul was unmoved by the thought of persecution. He didn't count his life dear to himself. He was a servant of the Lord, willing to lay his life down for the sake of the Gospel. He was building God's kingdom, not his own.

I once heard that Billy Graham said the turning point in his ministry came in 1949 while he was in

Los Angeles. The Lord spoke to him and said, "Billy, you make a very poor Holy Spirit." Billy Graham said that those words convicted him. He realized he'd been trying to persuade people to believe instead of allowing the Holy Spirit to draw them to the Father. He felt God was telling him to simplify. "I didn't call you to be the Holy Spirit," God said. "I only called you to speak the truth." It was reported that from then on, Billy Graham quit trying to convince people to believe. He just started proclaiming the truth and let the Holy Spirit do His job. He preached what he saw in Scripture and left the results with God. And what results they were!

When I started speaking and standing on the truth of the Word of God, I felt the recoil. My family thought I was crazy. Friends disowned me, and I got kicked out of church. Afterward I remember painting a house for a woman who attended a denominational church (the same denomination as the church I was kicked out of). As I witnessed to her while I worked, she asked, "Why did you ever leave this church? We need young men like you. You shouldn't have left."

"I didn't leave voluntarily," I said. "They asked me to leave when I received the baptism of the Holy Spirit."

"Are you talking about speaking in tongues?" she asked.

"That's part of it," I answered.

"They'd have kicked you out of my church too!" she declared.

So, I showed her the scripture in 1 Corinthians that says, *"Forbid not to speak with tongues"* (1 Cor. 14:39). "It's right here in the Bible," I said.

And, serious as a heart attack, she replied, "There are lots of things in the Bible we don't believe."

I didn't know how to respond to that. How do you talk to a person who doesn't care what the Bible has to say? Sadly, many Christians think this way. They've allowed the traditions of man (their church denomination) to nullify God's Word (Mark 7:8). They're not consistent or humble. They are moved by potential problems. They won't face the rejection and criticism that walking in humility—in faith—brings. But Paul said:

> *Be anxious for nothing, but in everything by prayer and supplication, with thanksgiving, let your requests be made known to God; and the peace of God, which surpasses all understanding, will guard your hearts and minds through Christ Jesus.*
>
> **Philippians 4:6–7, NKJV**

If we want to experience the peace of God, we have to *"be anxious for nothing."* We can't worry about the problems we may encounter tomorrow or about how people might respond. We have to humble ourselves and submit to God's Word, speaking and acting on the truth with consistency and love, and then leave the results to Him.

Back in 2009, the Lord told me I needed to do something to accommodate our Bible college. It was bursting at the seams and at the breaking point. I either needed to help it grow or kill it. Long story short, the Lord opened the door to 157 acres in Woodland Park, Colorado. The property came with a beautiful preexisting lodge, and as we stood on the deck praying for wisdom, I called the Realtor with an offer. He said, "There's another offer already on the table that's larger than yours. If you really want this property, we need to move now! I'll draw up the paperwork, but I'll need your signatures today or we'll lose it."

I'm not sure if what he said was true, but I told him, "I'm not in a hurry. If this is what God wants for us, we'll have it. If not, something better will come along. I'm not going to make a rash decision."

When one of the guys who was with me heard my response, he said, "I know this is God. If you were in the flesh—if this were something you were doing on your own—you would have responded differently. You would have felt the pressure to act now. That peace you've got is God." Needless to say, that was the property God had for us. We purchased it in September 2009 and named it The Sanctuary.

Casting his care upon God was how Paul remained steady in the face of persecution. He could have peace and finish his course with joy because he had died to self (Acts 20:24). When your life is all about you and your comfort, it's like being stuck on a treadmill—it's tiring, but you know if you stop moving,

❝ When your life is all about you and your comfort, it's like being stuck on a treadmill—it's tiring, but you know if you stop moving, you're going to get thrown."

you're going to get thrown, so you just keep going. It is so restful when you come to the end of yourself and begin responding to God instead of trying to get a response from God. That's what humility is all about.

Chapter Twenty-Six

GRACE IN TIME OF NEED

But he giveth more grace. Wherefore he saith, God resisteth the proud, but giveth grace unto the humble.

James 4:6

God gives grace and more grace to the humble. But His grace is not just to get you another promotion. Hebrews 4:16 tells us to come before God—and the only way to do that is in humility—to *"obtain mercy, and find grace to help in time of need."* The grace of God strengthens us. It empowers us to live above our circumstances and the persecution of this life to fulfill God's will. Paul said, *"For it is God which worketh in you both to will and to do of his good pleasure"* (Phil. 2:13). Here's how this verse was translated in the International Standard Version:

> *For it is God who is producing in you both the desire and the ability to do what pleases him.*

Aside from Jesus, Paul probably experienced more *"grace to help in time of need"* than any other person in Scripture. He was also one of the humblest. He depended upon God. He wasn't selfish or disobedient. He didn't seek his own glory or kingdom. He was a faithful witness who was thankful and consistent. And he said:

> *For though I would desire to glory, I shall not be a fool; for I will say the truth: but now I forbear, lest any man should think of me above that which he seeth me to be, or that he heareth of me. And lest I should be exalted above measure through the abundance of the revelations, there was given to me a thorn in the flesh, the messenger of Satan to buffet me, lest I should be exalted above measure.*

2 Corinthians 12:6–7

❝ He wasn't selfish or disobedient. He didn't seek his own glory or kingdom. He was a faithful witness who was thankful and consistent.❞

Most Christians misunderstand what Paul was saying here. They think he was prideful when he spoke of his *"abundance of revelations."* Thus, they equate his *"thorn in the flesh"* as the way God humbled him. That's wrong. Revelation from God does not cause pride. Knowledge puffs up (1 Cor. 8:1); revelation humbles. Paul was just speaking the truth. He *did* have an abundance of revelation. God had unlocked the Gospel of grace to him (Gal. 2:7). Paul would have been lying to deny that. It's because Paul was humble that he was able to receive these revelations from God.

Paul said his *"thorn in the flesh"* was a *"messenger of Satan."* It wasn't sickness. It wasn't a message from God warning Paul of his pride. God doesn't give us sickness. He doesn't cause divorces or business failures. The Bible teaches that afflictions and persecutions come to steal the Word (Mark 4:16-17). The phrase *"thorn in the flesh"* is a reference to persecution (Num. 33:55, Josh. 23:13, and Judg. 2:3). Paul's thorn was persecution. It was Satan doing everything he could to keep Paul's "abundance of revelations" quiet. Satan didn't want others to hear the amazing news of the Gospel, so he had Paul stoned, shipwrecked, beaten and whipped, thrown into prison, and constantly on the move because of threats to his life (2 Cor. 11:23–28). Paul called these things his "infirmities" (2 Cor. 11:30). But notice how he handled them:

> *For this thing I besought the Lord thrice, that it might depart from me. And he said unto me, My grace is sufficient for thee: for my strength is made perfect in weakness.*

> **2 Corinthians 12:8–9a**

Paul prayed. He went to the throne of grace to find mercy and help in his time of need (Heb. 4:16). And the Lord responded, *"My grace is sufficient for thee"* (2 Cor. 12:9). Paul went on, saying:

> *Most gladly therefore will I rather glory in my infirmities, that the power of Christ may rest upon me. Therefore I take pleasure in infirmities, in reproaches, in necessities, in persecutions, in distresses for Christ's sake: for when I am weak, then am I strong.*

2 Corinthians 12:9b–10

I once called a woman on the phone who answered my question of "How are you?" with "I'm weak in Him." That took me by surprise. Most people don't want to talk about their weaknesses. But when we recognize that we are weak, that we can do nothing in ourselves, that is when we are strong. As long as we read our own press releases and are confident in our own abilities, we are vulnerable to pride (Prov. 16:18). But if we will recognize that only by the grace of God can we accomplish anything of lasting value, that puts us into a position of strength. (This is one of the ways to know if you are doing what God's called you to do—God always calls believers to something beyond themselves.)

To the natural mind, it is foolishness to be both weak and strong at the same time. But to the humble, it is grace. When we depend on God—when we are humble—we allow His strength to work on our behalf (2 Chr. 16:9). Paul understood this. He understood that the purpose of grace was to help us in time of need. The problem is, most Christians just visit humility. They wait until they are pushed into a corner and circumstances look overwhelming before they humble themselves and run to the throne of grace. This is the main reason people struggle with depression. They look for the physical, chemical reasons for depression, not realizing that the true "organic" solution is humility.

Depressed people are entirely self-focused. They can only see what they don't have. When others prosper, they think, *Why not me?* instead of rejoicing with them. That's pride.

We used to sing a song called "Count Your Blessings." It went like this:

> *Count your blessings, name them one by one,*
> *Count your blessings, see what God has done!*
> *Count your blessings, name them one by one,*
> *Count your many blessings, see what God has done.*
> —Johnson Oatman Jr.

As a kid, I remember people standing up in church to testify how that song ministered to them. I remember one lady talking about how she complained about the pain in her feet—until she saw a person without any feet! Then she realized how blessed she was, and her attitude changed. If people suffering with depression would take this attitude and change their focus, they would be surprised at how good their life really is. If they would humble themselves and approach the throne of grace with confidence (faith), they would receive the grace to overcome.

I heard it said that the night before Mary, Queen of Scots was beheaded, her long red hair turned white from fear and worry. If that is true, she experienced a profound chemical imbalance. But it wasn't the chemical imbalance that caused her to fear and worry. It was the fear and worry that caused her chemical imbalance.

The same is true for depression. I don't doubt that people with depression have a chemical imbalance, but it's not the chemical issue that causes their depression. Their depression—a negative focus on self—causes the chemical issue. Either these people can take a pill to treat the symptom of depression, or they can get to the root of the problem through humility and beat it.

It is impossible to be depressed if your mind is stayed upon all Jesus has done for you. I don't care how bad your situation is, Jesus loved you enough to leave heaven and become a man. He loved you enough to suffer through rejection and murder. And He loved you enough to return from the grave and give you access to His grace by faith (Rom. 5:2). You have access. Grace belongs to you. It is only waiting for you to humble yourself and find it at His throne.

Living every day in humility and thankfulness is how we receive more grace from God. I'm not the most gifted person out there, but God has shown Himself strong in my weakness by surrounding me

❝Grace belongs to you. It is only waiting for you to humble yourself and find it at His throne.❞

with some of the most talented people I've ever met. Often as we discuss ways to fulfill the ministry's vision, they'll begin throwing out business terms that I don't understand. I'll have to call a time-out to ask questions.

I know I'm not the sharpest knife in the drawer or the smartest guy in the room, but God has graced me to do what I'm doing. And I've learned that instead of trying to fake it and impress those around me, all I need to do is rest in that grace. It's a position of strength to recognize that God has called me to teach the Word and others to manage the business and legal side of the ministry. As long as I humble myself and stick with what God told me to do, He will provide the grace—the people to help—to do what I'm *not* called to do. All I have to do is cooperate with God.

We need more grace to do the things and be the people God has called us to be. And praise God, God has already made that grace available to us (2 Pet. 1:3). All we have to do is humble ourselves and receive (James 4:6).

Father, we love You, and we receive with meekness the engrafted Word, which is able to save our souls (James 1:21). Though this teaching goes against everything we see in our culture, help us to see that this is not a message of rejection. It's a message of love and discipline. For what father does not disciple or correct the ones he loves (Heb. 12:7)? Father, we know that You love us. We know You want to pour Your grace upon us, so we humble ourselves and choose to cooperate with Your laws. We cast our care for our families, our jobs, and our futures on You. We trust You to deal with them. Lord, we renounce pride, and we choose to present our bodies to You as a living sacrifice (Rom. 12:1). Teach us to be thankful. Teach us to be faithful witnesses and to rest in Your unchanging goodness. Thank You for the grace to make course corrections as needed. We love You, and we ask these things knowing that You hear us (1 John 5:14–15). In Jesus's name, amen.

RECEIVE JESUS AS YOUR SAVIOR

Choosing to receive Jesus Christ as your Lord and Savior is the most important decision you'll ever make!

God's Word promises that *"if thou shalt confess with thy mouth the Lord Jesus, and shalt believe in thine heart that God hath raised him from the dead, thou shalt be saved. For with the heart man believeth unto righteousness; and with the mouth confession is made unto salvation"* (Rom. 10:9-10). *"For whosoever shall call upon the name of the Lord shall be saved"* (Rom. 10:13).

By His grace, God has already done everything to provide salvation. Your part is simply to believe and receive.

Pray out loud, "Jesus, I confess that You are my Lord and Savior. I believe in my heart that God raised You from the dead. By faith in Your Word, I receive salvation now. Thank You for saving me!"

The very moment you commit your life to Jesus Christ, the truth of His Word instantly comes to pass in your spirit. Now that you're born again, there's a brand-new you!

Please contact our Helpline (719-635-1111) and let us know that you've prayed to receive Jesus as your Savior. We would like to rejoice with you and help you understand more fully what has taken place in your life. We'll send you a free gift that will help you understand and grow in your new relationship with the Lord. Welcome to your new life!

RECEIVE THE HOLY SPIRIT

As His child, your loving heavenly Father wants to give you the supernatural power you need to live this new life.

> *For every one that asketh receiveth; and he that seeketh findeth; and to him that knocketh it shall be opened. . . . How much more shall your heavenly Father give the Holy Spirit to them that ask him?*
>
> **Luke 11:10 and 13b**

All you have to do is ask, believe, and receive!

Pray, "Father, I recognize my need for Your power to live this new life. Please fill me with Your Holy Spirit. By faith, I receive it right now! Thank You for baptizing me. Holy Spirit, You are welcome in my life!"

Congratulations! Now you're filled with God's supernatural power!

Some syllables from a language you don't recognize will rise up from your heart to your mouth (1 Cor. 14:14). As you speak them out loud by faith, you're releasing God's power from within and building yourself up in your spirit (1 Cor. 14:4). You can do this whenever and wherever you like.

It doesn't really matter whether you felt anything or not when you prayed to receive the Lord and His Spirit. If you believed in your heart that you received, then God's Word promises that you did. *"Therefore I say unto you, What things soever ye desire, when ye pray, believe that ye receive them, and ye shall have them"* (Mark 11:24). God always honors His Word—believe it!

Please contact our Helpline (719-635-1111) and let us know that you've prayed to be filled with the Holy Spirit. We would like to rejoice with you and help you understand more fully what has taken place in your life. We'll send you a free gift that will help you understand and grow in your new relationship with the Lord.

ABOUT THE AUTHOR

Andrew Wommack's life was forever changed the moment he encountered the supernatural love of God on March 23, 1968. As a renowned Bible teacher and author, Andrew has made it his mission to change the way the world sees God.

Andrew's vision is to go as far and deep with the Gospel as possible. His message goes far through the *Gospel Truth* television program, which is available to nearly half the world's population. The message goes deep through discipleship at Charis Bible College, headquartered in Woodland Park, Colorado. Founded in 1994, Charis has campuses across the United States and around the globe.

Andrew also has an extensive library of teaching materials in print, audio, and video—most of which can be accessed for free from his website: **awmi.net**.

CONTACT INFORMATION

Andrew Wommack Ministries Inc.

PO Box 3333

Colorado Springs CO 80934-3333

Email: info@awmi.net

Helpline: 719-635-1111

Helpline Hours: Monday through Friday,
twenty-four hours a day (MT)

awmi.net

Andrew's
LIVING
COMMENTARY
BIBLE SOFTWARE

Grow in the Word with Andrew through his *Living Commentary,* the most comprehensive accumulation of the revelation the Lord has given Andrew over the last fifty years.

The *Living Commentary* is a Bible software program for Windows and Mac that includes decades of Andrew Wommack's personal study notes on over 23,000 scriptures and counting. This "living" commentary is continually expanded as Andrew's recent studies are added to the program. Andrew's *Living Commentary* makes in-depth Bible study easier than ever before. The program allows you to compare scriptures and notes simply by hovering over a reference and includes several Bible versions, additional commentaries, dictionaries, concordances, maps, and other resources.

The *Living Commentary* also includes all the notes from Andrew's *Life for Today Study Bibles,* and an online version of *Living Commentary* can be accessed via devices with an up-to-date web browser.

The *Living Commentary* Bible software includes:

Bibles:
American Standard Version
American King James Version
Darby Bible Translation
Douay-Rheims Bible
English Revised Version
King James Version
King James Advanced Version
Webster Bible Translation
Weymouth New Testament
World English Bible
Young's Literal Translation

Word Studies:
Strong's Concordance
Englishman's Concordance
The Treasury of Scripture
  Knowledge

Commentaries:
Andrew Wommack's
• *Living Commentary*
• *Life for Today Study Bible and Commentary*
Adam Clarke's Commentary on the Bible
Albert Barnes' Notes on the Whole Bible
Matthew Henry's Concise Commentary

Dictionaries:
Oxford English Dictionary

Other Features:
User Notes
Book Introductions
Resources – Images, Maps, and More

Minimum System Requirements: Windows 7, 8, or 10; MacOS X 10.12 or greater.

Item Code: 8350
Price: $120
(This is not a suggested donation.)

719-635-1111 | awmi.net/LC